A Dictionary of

IT Service M

Terms, Definitions a

ITIL® 2011 Edition, '

GW01081451

Written by:	Ashley Hanna	HP
	Stuart Rance	HP
Edited by:	Mark Lillycrop itSMF UK	
Published by:	itSMF UK	

Based on previous editions of the dictionary by Ivor Evans, Ivor Macfarlane, Ashley Hanna and Stuart Rance.

ISBN 978-1-906745-05-9

Introduction

This new version of the Dictionary of IT Service Management is based on the ***ITIL® Glossary and Abbreviations,*** with additional service management definitions provided by the authors. The Glossary is also available to download under a clickable re-use licence at www.best-management-practice.com/

Terms without an asterisk (*) are taken directly from the ***ITIL® Glossary and Abbreviations***. Other terms commonly used within IT service management are highlighted with an asterisk (*).

The publication names included in parentheses after the name of an ITIL term identify where a reader can find more information about that term within a core ITIL 2011 publication. This is either because the term is primarily used by that publication or because additional useful information about that term can be found there. Terms without a publication name associated with them may be used generally by several publications, or may not be defined in any greater detail than can be found in the glossary, i.e. readers are only pointed to publications where they can expect to expand on their knowledge or to see a broader context. Terms with multiple publication names are expanded on in multiple publications.

A list of abbreviations and associated terms is provided at the end of the dictionary.

acceptance
Formal agreement that an IT service, process, plan or other deliverable is complete, accurate, reliable and meets its specified requirements. Acceptance is usually preceded by change evaluation or testing and is often required before proceeding to the next stage of a project or process.
See also *service acceptance criteria.*

access management
(ITIL Service Operation) The process responsible for allowing users to make use of IT services, data or other assets. Access management helps to protect the confidentiality, integrity and availability of assets by ensuring that only authorized users are able to access or modify them. Access management implements the policies of information security management and is sometimes referred to as rights management or identity management.

account manager
(ITIL Service Strategy) A role that is very similar to that of the business relationship manager, but includes more commercial aspects. Most commonly used by Type III service providers when dealing with external customers.

accounting
(ITIL Service Strategy) The process responsible for identifying the actual costs of delivering IT services, comparing these with budgeted costs, and managing variance from the budget.

accounting period
(ITIL Service Strategy) A period of time (usually one year) for which budgets, charges, depreciation and other financial calculations are made.
See also *financial year.*

accredited
Officially authorized to carry out a role. For example, an accredited body may be authorized to provide training or to conduct audits.

active monitoring
(ITIL Service Operation) Monitoring of a configuration item or an IT service that uses automated regular checks to discover the current status.
See also *passive monitoring.*

activity
A set of actions designed to achieve a particular result. Activities are usually defined as part of processes or plans, and are documented in procedures.

agreed service time (AST)
(ITIL Service Design) A synonym for service hours, commonly used in formal calculations of availability.
See also *downtime.*

agreement
A document that describes a formal understanding between two or more parties. An agreement is not legally binding, unless it forms part of a contract.
See also operational level agreement; service level agreement.

alert
(ITIL Service Operation) A notification that a threshold has been reached, something has changed, or a failure has occurred. Alerts are often created and managed by system management tools and are managed by the event management process.

analytical modelling
(ITIL Continual Service Improvement) (ITIL Service Design) (ITIL Service Strategy) A technique that uses mathematical models to predict the behaviour of IT services or other configuration items. Analytical models are commonly used in capacity management and availability management.
See also *modelling; simulation modelling.*

application
Software that provides functions which are required by an IT service. Each application may be part of more than one IT service. An application runs on one or more servers or clients.
See also *application management; application portfolio.*

application management
(ITIL Service Operation) The function responsible for managing applications throughout their lifecycle.

application portfolio

(ITIL Service Design) A database or structured document used to manage applications throughout their lifecycle. The application portfolio contains key attributes of all applications. The application portfolio is sometimes implemented as part of the service portfolio, or as part of the configuration management system.

application service provider (ASP)

(ITIL Service Design) An external service provider that provides IT services using applications running at the service provider's premises. Users access the applications by network connections to the service provider.

application sizing

(ITIL Service Design) The activity responsible for understanding the resource requirements needed to support a new application, or a major change to an existing application. Application sizing helps to ensure that the IT service can meet its agreed service level targets for capacity and performance.

architecture

(ITIL Service Design) The structure of a system or IT service, including the relationships of components to each other and to the environment they are in. Architecture also includes the standards and guidelines that guide the design and evolution of the system.

assembly

(ITIL Service Transition) A configuration item that is made up of a number of other CIs. For example, a server CI may contain CIs for CPUs, disks, memory etc.; an IT service CI may contain many hardware, software and other CIs.
See also *build; component CI. assessment.*

assessment

Inspection and analysis to check whether a standard or set of guidelines is being followed, that records are accurate, or that efficiency and effectiveness targets are being met.
See also *audit.*

asset

(ITIL Service Strategy) Any resource or capability. The assets of a service provider include anything that could contribute to the delivery of a service. Assets can be one of the following types: management, organization, process, knowledge, people, information, applications, infrastructure or financial capital.
See also *customer asset; service asset; strategic asset.*

asset management

(ITIL Service Transition) A generic activity or process responsible for tracking and reporting the value and ownership of assets throughout their lifecycle.
See also *service asset and configuration management; fixed asset management; software asset management.*

asset register

(ITIL Service Transition) A list of fixed assets that includes their ownership and value.
See also *fixed asset management.*

asset specificity

(ITIL Service Strategy) One or more attributes of an asset that make it particularly useful for a given purpose. Asset specificity may limit the use of the asset for other purposes.

attribute

(ITIL Service Transition) A piece of information about a configuration item. Examples are name, location, version number and cost. Attributes of CIs are recorded in a configuration management database (CMDB) and maintained as part of a configuration management system (CMS).
See also *relationship; configuration management system.*

audit

Formal inspection and verification to check whether a standard or set of guidelines is being followed, that records are accurate, or that efficiency and effectiveness targets are being met. An audit may be carried out by internal or external groups.
See also *assessment; certification.*

authority matrix

See *RACI.*

automatic call distribution (ACD)

(ITIL Service Operation) Use of information technology to direct an incoming telephone call to the most appropriate person in the shortest possible time. ACD is sometimes called automated call distribution.

availability

Ability of an IT service or other configuration item to perform its agreed function when required. Availability is determined by reliability, maintainability, serviceability, performance and security. Availability is usually calculated as a percentage. This calculation is often based on agreed service time and downtime. It is best practice to calculate availability of an IT service using measurements of the business output. availability management (AM).

availability management

(ITIL Service Design) The process responsible for ensuring that IT services meet the current and future availability needs of the business in a cost-effective and timely manner. Availability management defines, analyses, plans, measures and improves all aspects of the availability of IT services, and ensures that all IT infrastructures, processes, tools, roles etc. are appropriate for the agreed service level targets for availability.
See also *availability management information system. availability management information system (AMIS).*

availability management information system (AMIS)

(ITIL Service Design) A set of tools, data and information that is used to support availability management.
See also *service knowledge management system.*

availability plan

(ITIL Service Design) A plan to ensure that existing and future availability requirements for IT services can be provided cost-effectively.

B

back-office / back-end *
Business processes or functions that are not directly visible to business customers. For example order processing, shipping, receiving.

back-out
(ITIL Service Transition) An activity that restores a service or other configuration item to a previous baseline. Back-out is used as a form of remediation when a change or release is not successful. backup

backup
(ITIL Service Design) (ITIL Service Operation) Copying data to protect against loss of integrity or availability of the original.

balanced scorecard
(ITIL Continual Service Improvement) A management tool developed by Drs Robert Kaplan (Harvard Business School) and David Norton. A balanced scorecard enables a strategy to be broken down into key performance indicators. Performance against the KPIs is used to demonstrate how well the strategy is being achieved. A balanced scorecard has four major areas, each of which has a small number of KPIs. The same four areas are considered at different levels of detail throughout the organization.

baseline
(ITIL Continual Service Improvement) (ITIL Service Transition) A snapshot that is used as a reference point. Many snapshots may be taken and recorded over time but only some will be used as baselines. For example: an ITSM baseline can be used as a starting point to measure the effect of a service improvement plan; a performance baseline can be used to measure changes in performance over the lifetime of an IT service; a configuration baseline can be used as part of a back-out plan to enable the IT infrastructure to be restored to a known configuration if a change or release fails.
See also *benchmark.*

batch processing *
Processing a set of related computer programmes, transactions or documents together as a unit. Batch processing is often done outside of normal working hours, and may be scheduled and managed by IT operations control.

benchmark

(ITIL Continual Service Improvement) (ITIL Service Transition) A baseline that is used to compare related data sets as part of a benchmarking exercise. For example, a recent snapshot of a process can be compared to a previous baseline of that process, or a current baseline can be compared to industry data or best practice.
See also **benchmarking; baseline.**

benchmarking

(ITIL Continual Service Improvement) The process responsible for comparing a benchmark with related data sets such as a more recent snapshot, industry data or best practice. The term is also used to mean creating a series of benchmarks over time, and comparing the results to measure progress or improvement. This process is not described in detail within the core ITIL publications.

Best Management Practice (BMP)

The Best Management Practice portfolio is owned by the Cabinet Office, part of HM Government. Formerly owned by CCTA and then OGC, the BMP functions moved to the Cabinet Office in June 2010. The BMP portfolio includes guidance on IT service management and project, programme, risk, portfolio and value management. There is also a management maturity model as well as related glossaries of terms.

best practice

Proven activities or processes that have been successfully used by multiple organizations. ITIL is an example of best practice.

billing

(ITIL Service Strategy) Part of the charging process. Billing is the activity responsible for producing an invoice or a bill and recovering the money from customers.
See also **pricing.**

brainstorming

(ITIL Service Design) (ITIL Service Operation) A technique that helps a team to generate ideas. Ideas are not reviewed during the brainstorming session, but at a later stage. Brainstorming is often used by problem management to identify possible causes.

British Standards Institution (BSI)
The UK national standards body, responsible for creating and maintaining British standards. See www.bsi-global.com for more information.
See also *International Organization for Standardization.*

budget
A list of all the money an organization or business unit plans to receive, and plans to pay out, over a specified period of time.
See also *budgeting; planning.*

budgeting
The activity of predicting and controlling the spending of money. Budgeting consists of a periodic negotiation cycle to set future budgets (usually annual) and the day-to-day monitoring and adjusting of current budgets.

build
(ITIL Service Transition) The activity of assembling a number of configuration items to create part of an IT service. The term is also used to refer to a release that is authorized for distribution – for example, server build or laptop build. See also *configuration baseline.*

build environment
(ITIL Service Transition) A controlled environment where applications, IT services and other builds are assembled prior to being moved into a test or live environment.

business
(ITIL Service Strategy) An overall corporate entity or organization formed of a number of business units. In the context of ITSM, the term includes public sector and not-for-profit organizations, as well as companies. An IT service provider provides IT services to a customer within a business. The IT service provider may be part of the same business as its customer (internal service provider), or part of another business (external service provider).

business / IT alignment *
An approach to the delivery of IT services that tries to align the activities of the IT service provider with the needs of the business. More recent approaches such as ITIL V3 focus on business / IT integration, rather than on simple alignment.

business capacity management

(ITIL Continual Service Improvement) (ITIL Service Design) In the context of ITSM, business capacity management is the subprocess of capacity management responsible for understanding future business requirements for use in the capacity plan. See also service capacity management; component capacity management.

business case

(ITIL Service Strategy) Justification for a significant item of expenditure. The business case includes information about costs, benefits, options, issues, risks and possible problems.
See also cost *benefit analysis.*

business continuity management (BCM)

(ITIL Service Design) The business process responsible for managing risks that could seriously affect the business. Business continuity management safeguards the interests of key stakeholders, reputation, brand and value-creating activities. The process involves reducing risks to an acceptable level and planning for the recovery of business processes should a disruption to the business occur. Business continuity management sets the objectives, scope and requirements for IT service continuity management.

business continuity plan (BCP)

(ITIL Service Design) A plan defining the steps required to restore business processes following a disruption. The plan also identifies the triggers for invocation, people to be involved, communications etc. IT service continuity plans form a significant part of business continuity plans.

business continuity plan framework *

A template, set of guidelines, or set of outline plans used for creating multiple business continuity plans. BCP frameworks are most often used in organisations which need to produce plans covering many locations or business functions.

business customer

(ITIL Service Strategy) A recipient of a product or a service from the business. For example, if the business is a car manufacturer, then the business customer is someone who buys a car.

business impact analysis (BIA)

(ITIL Service Strategy) Business impact analysis is the activity in business continuity management that identifies vital business functions and their dependencies. These dependencies may include suppliers, people, other business processes, IT services etc. Business impact analysis defines the recovery requirements for IT services. These requirements include recovery time objectives, recovery point objectives and minimum service level targets for each IT service.

business objective

(ITIL Service Strategy) The objective of a business process, or of the business as a whole. Business objectives support the business vision, provide guidance for the IT strategy, and are often supported by IT services.

business operations

(ITIL Service Strategy) The day-to-day execution, monitoring and management of business processes.

business perspective

(ITIL Continual Service Improvement) An understanding of the service provider and IT services from the point of view of the business, and an understanding of the business from the point of view of the service provider.

business process

A process that is owned and carried out by the business. A business process contributes to the delivery of a product or service to a business customer. For example, a retailer may have a purchasing process that helps to deliver services to its business customers. Many business processes rely on IT services.

business recovery *

Reinstating business processes as part of a business continuity plan.

business relationship management

(ITIL Service Strategy) The process responsible for maintaining a positive relationship with customers. Business relationship management identifies customer needs and ensures that the service provider is able to meet these needs with an appropriate catalogue of services. This process has strong links with service level management.

business relationship manager

(ITIL Service Strategy) A role responsible for maintaining the relationship with one or more customers. This role is often combined with the service level manager role.

business representative *

Synonym for customer, usually used to refer to a manager in the customer organization who is responsible for communication with the service provider. See *informed customer.*

business service

A service that is delivered to business customers by business units. For example, delivery of financial services to customers of a bank, or goods to the customers of a retail store. Successful delivery of business services often depends on one or more IT services. A business service may consist almost entirely of an IT service – for example, an online banking service or an external website where product orders can be placed by business customers. See also *customer-facing service.*

business service management

A service that is delivered to business customers by business units. For example, delivery of financial services to customers of a bank, or goods to the customers of a retail store. Successful delivery of business services often depends on one or more IT services. A business service may consist almost entirely of an IT service – for example, an online banking service or an external website where product orders can be placed by business customers. See also *customer-facing service.*

business unit

(ITIL Service Strategy) A segment of the business that has its own plans, metrics, income and costs. Each business unit owns assets and uses these to create value for customers in the form of goods and services.

C

call
(ITIL Service Operation) A telephone call to the service desk from a user. A call could result in an incident or a service request being logged.

call centre
(ITIL Service Operation) An organization or business unit that handles large numbers of incoming and outgoing telephone calls.
See also *service desk.*

call type
(ITIL Service Operation) A category that is used to distinguish incoming requests to a service desk. Common call types are incident, service request and complaint.

capability
(ITIL Service Strategy) The ability of an organization, person, process, application, IT service or other configuration item to carry out an activity. Capabilities are intangible assets of an organization.
See also *resource.*

Capability Maturity Model Integration (CMMI)
Capability Maturity Model Integration (CMMI) (ITIL Continual Service Improvement) A process improvement approach developed by the Software Engineering Institute (SEI) of Carnegie Mellon University, US. CMMI provides organizations with the essential elements of effective processes. It can be used to guide process improvement across a project, a division or an entire organization. CMMI helps integrate traditionally separate organizational functions, set process improvement goals and priorities, provide guidance for quality processes, and provide a point of reference for appraising current processes. See www.sei.cmu.edu/cmmi for more information.
See also *maturity.*

capacity
(ITIL Service Design) The maximum throughput that a configuration item or IT service can deliver. For some types of CI, capacity may be the size or volume - for example, a disk drive.

capacity management
(ITIL Continual Service Improvement) (ITIL Service Design) The process responsible for ensuring that the capacity of IT services and the IT infrastructure is able to meet agreed capacity- and performance-related requirements in a cost-effective and timely manner. Capacity management considers all resources required to deliver an IT service, and is concerned with meeting both the current and future capacity and performance needs of the business. Capacity management includes three sub-processes: business capacity management, service capacity management, and component capacity management.
See also **capacity management information system.**

capacity management database *
A database containing all data needed to support capacity management.
See capacity **management Information system.**

capacity management information system (CMIS)
(ITIL Service Design) A set of tools, data and information that is used to support capacity management.
See also **service knowledge management system.**

capacity plan
(ITIL Service Design) A plan used to manage the resources required to deliver IT services. The plan contains details of current and historic usage of IT services and components, and any issues that need to be addressed (including related improvement activities). The plan also contains scenarios for different predictions of business demand and costed options to deliver the agreed service level targets.

capacity planning
(ITIL Service Design) The activity within capacity management responsible for creating a capacity plan..

capital budgeting
(ITIL Service Strategy) The present commitment of funds in order to receive a return in the future in the form of additional cash inflows or reduced cash outflows.

capital cost
(ITIL Service Strategy) The cost of purchasing something that will become a financial asset – for example, computer equipment and buildings. The value of the asset depreciates over multiple accounting periods.
See also **operational cost.**

capital expenditure (CAPEX)
See *capital cost.*

capital item *
Synonym for fixed asset.

capitalization
(ITIL Service Strategy) Identifying major cost as capital, even though no asset is purchased. This is done to spread the impact of the cost over multiple accounting periods. The most common example of this is software development, or purchase of a software licence.

category
A named group of things that have something in common. Categories are used to group similar things together. For example, cost types are used to group similar types of cost. Incident categories are used to group similar types of incident, while CI types are used to group similar types of configuration item.

cause / effect diagram *
Synonym for Ishikawa diagram

CCTA risk analysis & management method *
See *CRAMM.*

certification
Issuing a certificate to confirm compliance to a standard. Certification includes a formal audit by an independent and accredited body. The term is also used to mean awarding a certificate to provide evidence that a person has achieved a qualification.

change
(ITIL Service Transition) The addition, modification or removal of anything that could have an effect on IT services. The scope should include changes to all architectures, processes, tools, metrics and documentation, as well as changes to IT services and other configuration items.

change advisory board (CAB)
(ITIL Service Transition) A group of people that support the assessment, prioritization, authorization and scheduling of changes. A change advisory board is usually made up of representatives from: all areas within the IT service provider; the business; and third parties such as suppliers.

change advisory board / emergency committee *
Synonym for emergency change advisory board (ECAB).

change authority *
A role, person or group that provides formal approval for a change. There may be multiple change authorities, with different levels of approval. In many organisations a change manager or change advisory board (CAB) acts as a change authority.

change control *
A limited change management process. Change control typically includes approval of changes after they have been planned and designed, but does not manage the whole lifecycle of the change.

change evaluation
(ITIL Service Transition) The process responsible for formal assessment of a new or changed IT service to ensure that risks have been managed and to help determine whether to authorize the change.

change history
(ITIL Service Transition) Information about all changes made to a configuration item during its life. Change history consists of all those change records that apply to the CI.

change management
(ITIL Service Transition) The process responsible for controlling the lifecycle of all changes, enabling beneficial changes to be made with minimum disruption to IT services.

change model
(ITIL Service Transition) A repeatable way of dealing with a particular category of change. A change model defines specific agreed steps that will be followed for a change of this category. Change models may be very complex with many steps that require authorization (e.g. major software release) or may be very simple with no requirement for authorization (e.g. password reset).
See also *change advisory board; standard change.*

change proposal
(ITIL Service Strategy) (ITIL Service Transition) A document that includes a high level description of a potential service introduction or significant change, along with a corresponding business case and an expected implementation schedule. Change proposals are normally created by the service portfolio management process and are passed to change management for authorization. Change management will review the potential impact on other services, on shared resources, and on the overall change schedule. Once the change proposal has been authorized, service portfolio management will charter the service.

change record
(ITIL Service Transition) A record containing the details of a change. Each change record documents the lifecycle of a single change. A change record is created for every request for change that is received, even those that are subsequently rejected. Change records should reference the configuration items that are affected by the change. Change records may be stored in the configuration management system, or elsewhere in the service knowledge management system.

change request
See *request for change.*

change schedule
(ITIL Service Transition) A document that lists all authorized changes and their planned implementation dates, as well as the estimated dates of longer-term changes. A change schedule is sometimes called a forward schedule of change, even though it also contains information about changes that have already been implemented.

change slot *
Synonym for change window.

change window
(ITIL Service Transition) A regular, agreed time when changes or releases may be implemented with minimal impact on services. Change windows are usually documented in service level agreements.

chargeable item
(ITIL Service Strategy) A deliverable of an IT service that is used in calculating charges to customers (for example, number of transactions, number of desktop PCs).

charging

(ITIL Service Strategy) Requiring payment for IT services. Charging for IT services is optional, and many organizations choose to treat their IT service provider as a cost centre.
See also *charging process; charging policy.*

charging policy

(ITIL Service Strategy) A policy specifying the objective of the charging process and the way in which charges will be calculated.
See also *cost.*

charging process

(ITIL Service Strategy) The process responsible for deciding how much customers should pay (pricing) and recovering money from them (billing). This process is not described in detail within the core ITIL publications.

charter

(ITIL Service Strategy) A document that contains details of a new service, a significant change or other significant project. Charters are typically authorized by service portfolio management or by a project management office. The term charter is also used to describe the act of authorizing the work required to complete the service change or project.
See also *change proposal; service charter; project portfolio.*

chronological anaylsis

(ITIL Service Operation) A technique used to help identify possible causes of problems. All available data about the problem is collected and sorted by date and time to provide a detailed timeline. This can make it possible to identify which events may have been triggered by others.

CI type

(ITIL Service Transition) A category that is used to classify configuration items. The CI type identifies the required attributes and relationships for a configuration record. Common CI types include hardware, document, user etc.

classification

The act of assigning a category to something. Classification is used to ensure consistent management and reporting. Configuration items, incidents, problems, changes etc. are usually classified.

client

A generic term that means a customer, the business or a business customer. For example, client manager may be used as a synonym for business relationship manager. The term is also used to mean a computer that is used directly by a user – for example, a PC, a handheld computer or a work station; or the part of a client server application that the user directly interfaces with – for example, an email client.

closed

(ITIL Service Operation) The final status in the lifecycle of an incident, problem, change etc. When the status is closed, no further action is taken.

closure

(ITIL Service Operation) The act of changing the status of an incident, problem, change etc. to closed.

closure code *

A category assigned to an incident, problem, service request or change when it is closed. The closure code typically shows the true cause, resolution or outcome and is used for trend analysis and reporting.

COBIT

(ITIL Continual Service Improvement) Control OBjectives for Information and related Technology (COBIT) provides guidance and best practice for the management of IT processes. COBIT is published by ISACA in conjunction with the IT Governance Institute (ITGI). See www.isaca.org for more information.

code of practice

A guideline published by a public body or a standards organization, such as ISO or BSI. Many standards consist of a code of practice and a specification. The code of practice describes recommended best practice.

cold standby

See *gradual recovery.*

commercial off the shelf (COTS)

(ITIL Service Design) Pre-existing application software or middleware that can be purchased from a third party.

compliance

Ensuring that a standard or set of guidelines is followed, or that proper, consistent accounting or other practices are being employed.

component
A general term that is used to mean one part of something more complex. For example, a computer system may be a component of an IT service; an application may be a component of a release unit. Components that need to be managed should be configuration items.

component capacity management (CCM)
(ITIL Continual Service Improvement) (ITIL Service Design) The sub-process of capacity management responsible for understanding the capacity, utilization and performance of configuration items. Data is collected, recorded and analysed for use in the capacity plan.
See also *business capacity management; service capacity management.*

component CI
(ITIL Service Transition) A configuration item that is part of an assembly. For example, a CPU or memory CI may be part of a server CI.

component failure impact analysis (CFIA)
(ITIL Service Design) A technique that helps to identify the impact of configuration item failure on IT services and the business. A matrix is created with IT services on one axis and CIs on the other. This enables the identification of critical CIs (that could cause the failure of multiple IT services) and fragile IT services (that have multiple single points of failure).

computer telephony integration (CTI)
(ITIL Service Operation) Computer telephony integration is a general term covering any kind of integration between computers and telephone systems. It is most commonly used to refer to systems where an application displays detailed screens relating to incoming or outgoing telephone calls.
See also *automatic call distribution; interactive voice response.*

concurrency
A measure of the number of users engaged in the same operation at the same time.

confidentiality
(ITIL Service Design) A security principle that requires that data should only be accessed by authorized people.

configuration

(ITIL Service Transition) A generic term used to describe a group of configuration items that work together to deliver an IT service, or a recognizable part of an IT service. Configuration is also used to describe the parameter settings for one or more configuration items.

configuration baseline

(ITIL Service Transition) The baseline of a configuration that has been formally agreed and is managed through the change management process. A configuration baseline is used as a basis for future builds, releases and changes.

configuration control

(ITIL Service Transition) The activity responsible for ensuring that adding, modifying or removing a configuration item is properly managed – for example, by submitting a request for change or service request.

configuration identification

(ITIL Service Transition) The activity responsible for collecting information about configuration items and their relationships, and loading this information into the configuration management database. Configuration identification is also responsible for labelling the configuration items themselves, so that the corresponding configuration records can be found.

configuration item (CI)

(ITIL Service Transition) Any component or other service asset that needs to be managed in order to deliver an IT service. Information about each configuration item is recorded in a configuration record within the configuration management system and is maintained throughout its lifecycle by service asset and configuration management. Configuration items are under the control of change management. They typically include IT services, hardware, software, buildings, people and formal documentation such as process documentation and service level agreements.

configuration management

See **service asset and configuration management.**

configuration management database (CMDB)

(ITIL Service Transition) A database used to store configuration records throughout their lifecycle. The configuration management system maintains one or more configuration management databases, and each database stores attributes of configuration items, and relationships with other configuration items.

configuration management system (CMS)

(ITIL Service Transition) A set of tools, data and information that is used to support service asset and configuration management. The CMS is part of an overall service knowledge management system and includes tools for collecting, storing, managing, updating, analysing and presenting data about all configuration items and their relationships. The CMS may also include information about incidents, problems, known errors, changes and releases. The CMS is maintained by service asset and configuration management and is used by all IT service management processes.
See also *configuration management database.*

configuration record

(ITIL Service Transition) A record containing the details of a configuration item. Each configuration record documents the lifecycle of a single configuration item. Configuration records are stored in a configuration management database and maintained as part of a configuration management system.

configuration structure

(ITIL Service Transition) The hierarchy and other relationships between all the configuration items that comprise a configuration.

configuration verification *

Activities that verify configuration data is accurate.
See *verification and audit.*

contingency planning *

Planning to deal with specific risks. Contingency planning may be included in any process, activity or plan, but is most often seen as part of risk management and IT service continuity management.

continual service improvement (CSI)
(ITIL Continual Service Improvement) A stage in the lifecycle of a service. Continual service improvement ensures that services are aligned with changing business needs by identifying and implementing improvements to IT services that support business processes. The performance of the IT service provider is continually measured and improvements are made to processes, IT services and IT infrastructure in order to increase efficiency, effectiveness and cost effectiveness. Continual service improvement includes the seven-step improvement process. Although this process is associated with continual service improvement, most processes have activities that take place across multiple stages of the service lifecycle.
See also *Plan-Do-Check-Act.*

continual service improvement programme (CSIP) *
A formal programme to implement and manage a continual service improvement process.

continuous availability
(ITIL Service Design) An approach or design to achieve 100% availability. A continuously available IT service has no planned or unplanned downtime.

continuous operation
(ITIL Service Design) An approach or design to eliminate planned downtime of an IT service. Note that individual configuration items may be down even though the IT service is available.

contract
A legally binding agreement between two or more parties.

control
A means of managing a risk, ensuring that a business objective is achieved or that a process is followed. Examples of control include policies, procedures, roles, RAID, door locks etc. A control is sometimes called a countermeasure or safeguard. Control also means to manage the utilization or behaviour of a configuration item, system or IT service.

Control OBjectives for Information and related Technology
See *COBIT.*

control perspective

(ITIL Service Strategy) An approach to the management of IT services, processes, functions, assets etc. There can be several different control perspectives on the same IT service, process etc., allowing different individuals or teams to focus on what is important and relevant to their specific role. Examples of control perspective include reactive and proactive management within IT operations, or a lifecycle view for an application project team.

control processes

The ISO/IEC 20000 process group that includes change management and configuration management.

core service

(ITIL Service Strategy) A service that delivers the basic outcomes desired by one or more customers. A core service provides a specific level of utility and warranty. Customers may be offered a choice of utility and warranty through one or more service options.
See also *enabling service; enhancing service; IT service; service package.*

cost

The amount of money spent on a specific activity, IT service or business unit. Costs consist of real cost (money), notional cost (such as people's time) and depreciation.

cost benefit analysis

An activity that analyses and compares the costs and the benefits involved in one or more alternative courses of action. See also business case; internal rate of return; net present value; return on investment; value on investment.

cost centre

(ITIL Service Strategy) A business unit or project to which costs are assigned. A cost centre does not charge for services provided. An IT service provider can be run as a cost centre or a profit centre.

cost effectiveness

A measure of the balance between the effectiveness and cost of a service, process or activity. A cost-effective process is one that achieves its objectives at minimum cost.
See also *key performance indicator; return on investment; value for money.*

cost element

(ITIL Service Strategy) The middle level of category to which costs are assigned in budgeting and accounting. The highest-level category is cost type. For example, a cost type of 'people' could have cost elements of payroll, staff benefits, expenses, training, overtime etc. Cost elements can be further broken down to give cost units. For example, the cost element 'expenses' could include cost units of hotels, transport, meals etc.

cost management

(ITIL Service Strategy) A general term that is used to refer to budgeting and accounting, and is sometimes used as a synonym for financial management.

cost model

(ITIL Service Strategy) A framework used in budgeting and accounting in which all known costs can be recorded, categorized and allocated to specific customers, business units or projects. See also cost type; cost element; cost unit.

cost type

(ITIL Service Strategy) The highest level of category to which costs are assigned in budgeting and accounting – for example, hardware, software, people, accommodation, external and transfer.
See also *cost element; cost unit.*

cost unit

(ITIL Service Strategy) The lowest level of category to which costs are assigned, cost units are usually things that can be easily counted (e.g. staff numbers, software licences) or things easily measured (e.g. CPU usage, electricity consumed). Cost units are included within cost elements. For example, a cost element of 'expenses' could include cost units of hotels, transport, meals etc.
See also *cost type.*

countermeasure

Can be used to refer to any type of control. The term is most often used when referring to measures that increase resilience, fault tolerance or reliability of an IT service.

course corrections

Changes made to a plan or activity that has already started to ensure that it will meet its objectives. Course corrections are made as a result of monitoring progress.

CRAMM *
A methodology and tool for analysing and managing risks. CRAMM was developed by the UK Government, but is now privately owned. Further information is available from http://www.cramm.com/

crisis management
Crisis management is the process responsible for managing the wider implications of business continuity. A crisis management team is responsible for strategic issues such as managing media relations and shareholder confidence, and decides when to invoke business continuity plans.

critical success factor (CSF)
Something that must happen if an IT service, process, plan, project or other activity is to succeed. Key performance indicators are used to measure the achievement of each critical success factor. For example, a critical success factor of 'protect IT services when making changes' could be measured by key performance indicators such as 'percentage reduction of unsuccessful changes', 'percentage reduction in changes causing incidents' etc.

CSI register
(ITIL Continual Service Improvement) A database or structured document used to record and manage improvement opportunities throughout their lifecycle.

culture
A set of values that is shared by a group of people, including expectations about how people should behave, their ideas, beliefs and practices.
See also *vision.*

customer
Someone who buys goods or services. The customer of an IT service provider is the person or group who defines and agrees the service level targets. The term is also sometimes used informally to mean user – for example, 'This is a customer-focused organization.'

customer asset
Any resource or capability of a customer.
See also *asset.*

customer agreement portfolio

(ITIL Service Strategy) A database or structured document used to manage service contracts or agreements between an IT service provider and its customers. Each IT service delivered to a customer should have a contract or other agreement that is listed in the customer agreement portfolio.

See also *customer-facing service; service catalogue; service portfolio.*

customer portfolio

(ITIL Service Strategy) A database or structured document used to record all customers of the IT service provider. The customer portfolio is the business relationship manager's view of the customers who receive services from the IT service provider.

See also *customer agreement portfolio; service catalogue; service portfolio.*

customer-facing service

(ITIL Service Design) An IT service that is visible to the customer. These are normally services that support the customer's business processes and facilitate one or more outcomes desired by the customer. All live customer-facing services, including those available for deployment, are recorded in the service catalogue along with customer-visible information about deliverables, prices, contact points, ordering and request processes. Other information such as relationships to supporting services and other CIs will also be recorded for internal use by the IT service provider.

customer relationship management *

Synonym for business relationship management.

dashboard

(ITIL Service Operation) A graphical representation of overall IT service performance and availability. Dashboard images may be updated in real time, and can also be included in management reports and web pages. Dashboards can be used to support service level management, event management and incident diagnosis.

Data-to-Information-to-Knowledge-to-Wisdom (DIKW)

(ITIL Service Transition) A way of understanding the relationships between data, information, knowledge and wisdom. DIKW shows how each of these builds on the others.

definitive hardware store *

Synonym for spares store.

definitive media library (DML)

(ITIL Service Transition) One or more locations in which the definitive and authorized versions of all software configuration items are securely stored. The definitive media library may also contain associated configuration items such as licences and documentation. It is a single logical storage area even if there are multiple locations. The definitive media library is controlled by service asset and configuration management and is recorded in the configuration management system.

definitive software library *

Synonym for definitive media library (DML).

deliverable

Something that must be provided to meet a commitment in a service level agreement or a contract. It is also used in a more informal way to mean a planned output of any process.

demand management

(ITIL Service Design) (ITIL Service Strategy) The process responsible for understanding, anticipating and influencing customer demand for services. Demand management works with capacity management to ensure that the service provider has sufficient capacity to meet the required demand. At a strategic level, demand management can involve analysis of patterns of business activity and user profiles, while at a tactical level, it can involve the use of differential charging to encourage customers to use IT services at less busy times, or require short term activities to respond to unexpected demand or the failure of a configuration item.

Deming Cycle

See *Plan-Do-Check-Act.*

dependency

The direct or indirect reliance of one process or activity on another.

deployment

(ITIL Service Transition) The activity responsible for movement of new or changed hardware, software, documentation, process etc. to the live environment. Deployment is part of the release and deployment management process.

depreciation

(ITIL Service Strategy) A measure of the reduction in value of an asset over its life. This is based on wearing out, consumption or other reduction in the useful economic value.

design

(ITIL Service Design) An activity or process that identifies requirements and then defines a solution that is able to meet these requirements.
See also *service design.*

design coordination

(ITIL Service Design) The process responsible for coordinating all service design activities, processes and resources. Design coordination ensures the consistent and effective design of new or changed IT services, service management information systems, architectures, technology, processes, information and metrics.

detection

(ITIL Service Operation) A stage in the expanded incident lifecycle. Detection results in the incident becoming known to the service provider. Detection can be automatic or the result of a user logging an incident.

development

(ITIL Service Design) The process responsible for creating or modifying an IT service or application ready for subsequent release and deployment. Development is also used to mean the role or function that carries out development work. This process is not described in detail within the core ITIL publications.

development environment

(ITIL Service Design) An environment used to create or modify IT services or applications. Development environments are not typically subjected to the same degree of control as test or live environments.
See also *development.*

diagnosis

(ITIL Service Operation) A stage in the incident and problem lifecycles. The purpose of diagnosis is to identify a workaround for an incident or the root cause of a problem.

diagnostic script

(ITIL Service Operation) A structured set of questions used by service desk staff to ensure they ask the correct questions, and to help them classify, resolve and assign incidents. Diagnostic scripts may also be made available to users to help them diagnose and resolve their own incidents.

differential charging

A technique used to support demand management by charging different amounts for the same function of an IT service under different circumstances. For example, reduced charges outside peak times, or increased charges for users who exceed a bandwidth allocation.

direct cost

(ITIL Service Strategy) The cost of providing an IT service which can be allocated in full to a specific customer, cost centre, project etc. For example, the cost of providing nonshared servers or software licences.
See also *indirect cost.*

directory service
(ITIL Service Operation) An application that manages information about IT infrastructure available on a network, and corresponding user access rights.

disaster recovery *
Synonym for IT service continuity management.

do nothing *
A recovery option. The service provider formally agrees with the customer that recovery of this IT service will not be performed.

document
Information in readable form. A document may be paper or electronic – for example, a policy statement, service level agreement, incident record or diagram of a computer room layout.
See also *record.*

dormant contract *
A contract with a supplier to provide required products or services within agreed times at an agreed price. The contract is invoked as part of a recovery plan, at which time an additional payment is made and the goods or service are provided.

downtime
(ITIL Service Design) (ITIL Service Operation) The time when an IT service or other configuration item is not available during its agreed service time. The availability of an IT service is often calculated from agreed service time and downtime.

driver
Something that influences strategy, objectives or requirements – for example, new legislation or the actions of competitors.

duplex *
An availability management technique. Two, usually identical, components are used, each of which is capable of performing the full task if the other fails.
See *fault tolerance.*

early life support (ELS)
(ITIL Service Transition) A stage in the service lifecycle that occurs at the end of deployment and before the service is fully accepted into operation. During early life support, the service provider reviews key performance indicators, service levels and monitoring thresholds and may implement improvements to ensure that service targets can be met. The service provider may also provide additional resources for incident and problem management during this time.

economies of scale
(ITIL Service Strategy) The reduction in average cost that is possible from increasing the usage of an IT service or asset.
See also *economies of scope.*

economies of scope
(ITIL Service Strategy) The reduction in cost that is allocated to an IT service by using an existing asset for an additional purpose. For example, delivering a new IT service from an existing IT infrastructure.
See also *economies of scale.*

effectiveness
(ITIL Continual Service Improvement) A measure of whether the objectives of a process, service or activity have been achieved. An effective process or activity is one that achieves its agreed objectives.
See also *key performance indicator.*

efficiency
(ITIL Continual Service Improvement) A measure of whether the right amount of resource has been used to deliver a process, service or activity. An efficient process achieves its objectives with the minimum amount of time, money, people or other resources.
See also *key performance indicator.*

emergency change
(ITIL Service Transition) A change that must be introduced as soon as possible - for example, to resolve a major incident or implement a security patch. The change management process will normally have a specific procedure for handling emergency changes.
See also *emergency change advisory board.*

emergency change advisory board (ECAB)

(ITIL Service Transition) A subgroup of the change advisory board that makes decisions about emergency changes. Membership may be decided at the time a meeting is called, and depends on the nature of the emergency change.

enabling service

(ITIL Service Strategy) A service that is needed in order to deliver a core service. Enabling services may or may not be visible to the customer, but they are not offered to customers in their own right.
See also *enhancing service.*

enhancing service

(ITIL Service Strategy) A service that is added to a core service to make it more attractive to the customer. Enhancing services are not essential to the delivery of a core service but are used to encourage customers to use the core services or to differentiate the service provider from its competitors.
See also *enabling service; excitement factor.*

enterprise financial management

(ITIL Service Strategy) The function and processes responsible for managing the overall organization's budgeting, accounting and charging requirements. Enterprise financial management is sometimes referred to as the 'corporate' financial department.
See also *financial management for IT services.*

end-user *

Synonym for user.

environment

(ITIL Service Transition) A subset of the IT infrastructure that is used for a particular purpose – for example, live environment, test environment, build environment. Also used in the term 'physical environment' to mean the accommodation, air conditioning, power system etc. Environment is used as a generic term to mean the external conditions that influence or affect something.

error

(ITIL Service Operation) A design flaw or malfunction that causes a failure of one or more IT services or other configuration items. A mistake made by a person or a faulty process that impacts a configuration item is also an error.

escalation

(ITIL Service Operation) An activity that obtains additional resources when these are needed to meet service level targets or customer expectations. Escalation may be needed within any IT service management process, but is most commonly associated with incident management, problem management and the management of customer complaints. There are two types of escalation: functional escalation and hierarchic escalation.

eSourcing Capability Model for Client Organizations (eSCM-CL)

(ITIL Service Strategy) A framework to help organizations in their analysis and decisionmaking on service sourcing models and strategies. It was developed by Carnegie Mellon University in the US.
See also *eSourcing Capability Model for Service Providers.*

eSourcing Capability Model for Service Providers (eSCM-SP)

(ITIL Service Strategy) A framework to help IT service providers develop their IT service management capabilities from a service sourcing perspective. It was developed by Carnegie Mellon University in the US.
See also *eSourcing Capability Model for Client Organizations.*

estimation

The use of experience to provide an approximate value for a metric or cost. Estimation is also used in capacity and availability management as the cheapest and least accurate modelling method.

event

(ITIL Service Operation) A change of state that has significance for the management of an IT service or other configuration item. The term is also used to mean an alert or notification created by any IT service, configuration item or monitoring tool. Events typically require IT operations personnel to take actions, and often lead to incidents being logged.

event management

(ITIL Service Operation) The process responsible for managing events throughout their lifecycle. Event management is one of the main activities of IT operations.

exception report

A document containing details of one or more key performance indicators or other important targets that have exceeded defined thresholds. Examples include service level agreement targets being missed or about to be missed, and a performance metric indicating a potential capacity problem.

excitement attribute
See *excitement factor.*

excitement factor
(ITIL Service Strategy) An attribute added to something to make it more attractive or more exciting to the customer. For example, a restaurant may provide a free drink with every meal.
See also *enhancing service.*

expanded incident lifecycle
(ITIL Continual Service Improvement) (ITIL Service Design) Detailed stages in the lifecycle of an incident. The stages are detection, diagnosis, repair, recovery and restoration. The expanded incident lifecycle is used to help understand all contributions to the impact of incidents and to plan for how these could be controlled or reduced.

external customer
A customer who works for a different business from the IT service provider.
See also *external service provider; internal customer.*

external metric
A metric that is used to measure the delivery of IT service to a customer. External metrics are usually defined in service level agreements and reported to customers.
See also *internal metric.*

external service provider
(ITIL Service Strategy) An IT service provider that is part of a different organization from its customer. An IT service provider may have both internal and external customers.
See also *outsourcing; Type III service provider.*

external sourcing *
Synonym for outsourcing.

external target *
See *external metric.*

facilities management

(ITIL Service Operation) The function responsible for managing the physical environment where the IT infrastructure is located. Facilities management includes all aspects of managing the physical environment - for example, power and cooling, building access management, and environmental monitoring.

failure

(ITIL Service Operation) Loss of ability to operate to specification, or to deliver the required output. The term may be used when referring to IT services, processes, activities, configuration items etc. A failure often causes an incident.

Failure Modes and Effects Analysis (FMEA) *

An approach to assessing the potential impact of failures. FMEA involves analysing what would happen after failure of each configuration item, all the way up to the effect on the business. FMEA is often used in information security management and in IT service continuity planning.

fast recovery

(ITIL Service Design) A recovery option that is also known as hot standby. Fast recovery normally uses a dedicated fixed facility with computer systems and software configured ready to run the IT services. Fast recovery typically takes up to 24 hours but may be quicker if there is no need to restore data from backups.

fault

See *error.*

fault tolerance

(ITIL Service Design) The ability of an IT service or other configuration item to continue to operate correctly after failure of a component part.
See also *countermeasure; resilience.*

fault tree analysis (FTA)

(ITIL Continual Service Improvement) (ITIL Service Design) A technique that can be used to determine a chain of events that has caused an incident, or may cause an incident in the future. Fault tree analysis represents a chain of events using Boolean notation in a diagram.

financial management

(ITIL Service Strategy) A generic term used to describe the function and processes responsible for managing an organization's budgeting, accounting and charging requirements. Enterprise financial management is the specific term used to describe the function and processes from the perspective of the overall organization. Financial management for IT services is the specific term used to describe the function and processes from the perspective of the IT service provider.

financial management for IT services

(ITIL Service Strategy) The function and processes responsible for managing an IT service provider's budgeting, accounting and charging requirements. Financial management for IT services secures an appropriate level of funding to design, develop and deliver services that meet the strategy of the organization in a cost-effective manner.
See also *enterprise financial management.*

financial year

(ITIL Service Strategy) An accounting period covering 12 consecutive months. A financial year may start on any date (for example, 1 April to 31 March).

first level support *

Synonym for first-line support.

first time fix rate *

A metric that measures the percentage of incidents that are resolved during the initial user contact.

first-line support

(ITIL Service Operation) The first level in a hierarchy of support groups involved in the resolution of incidents. Each level contains more specialist skills, or has more time or other resources.
See also *escalation.*

fishbone diagram

See *Ishikawa diagram.*

fit for purpose
(ITIL Service Strategy) The ability to meet an agreed level of utility. Fit for purpose is also used informally to describe a process, configuration item, IT service etc. that is capable of meeting its objectives or service levels. Being fit for purpose requires suitable design, implementation, control and maintenance.

fit for use
(ITIL Service Strategy) The ability to meet an agreed level of warranty. Being fit for use requires suitable design, implementation, control and maintenance.

fixed asset
(ITIL Service Transition) A tangible business asset that has a long-term useful life (for example, a building, a piece of land, a server or a software licence).
See also *service asset; configuration item.*

fixed asset management
(ITIL Service Transition) The process responsible for tracking and reporting the value and ownership of fixed assets throughout their lifecycle. Fixed asset management maintains the asset register and is usually carried out by the overall business, rather than by the IT organization. Fixed asset management is sometimes called financial asset management and is not described in detail within the core ITIL publications.

fixed cost
(ITIL Service Strategy) A cost that does not vary with IT service usage – for example, the cost of server hardware.
See also *variable cost.*

fixed facility
(ITIL Service Design) A permanent building, available for use when needed by an IT service continuity plan.
See also *portable facility; recovery option.*

follow the sun
(ITIL Service Operation) A methodology for using service desks and support groups around the world to provide seamless 24/7 service. Calls, incidents, problems and service requests are passed between groups in different time zones.

fortress approach *

An approach to IT service continuity management where the main focus is risk prevention. A typical fortress approach attempts to prevent all major incidents. For example building a data centre with multiple perimeter walls and earthquake resistant construction.

forward schedule of change *

Synonym for change schedule

front-office / front-end *

Business processes or functions that are directly visible to business customers. For example sales or marketing.
See **back-office.**

fulfilment

Performing activities to meet a need or requirement - for example, by providing a new IT service, or meeting a service request.

function

A team or group of people and the tools or other resources they use to carry out one or more processes or activities - for example, the service desk. The term also has two other meanings: an intended purpose of a configuration item, person, team, process or IT service (for example, one function of an email service may be to store and forward outgoing mails, while the function of a business process may be to despatch goods to customers); or to perform the intended purpose correctly, as in 'The computer is functioning.'

functional escalation

(ITIL Service Operation) Transferring an incident, problem or change to a technical team with a higher level of expertise to assist in an escalation.

G

gap analysis

(ITIL Continual Service Improvement) An activity that compares two sets of data and identifies the differences. Gap analysis is commonly used to compare a set of requirements with actual delivery.

See also **benchmarking.**

governance

Ensures that policies and strategy are actually implemented, and that required processes are correctly followed. Governance includes defining roles and responsibilities, measuring and reporting, and taking actions to resolve any issues identified.

gradual recovery

(ITIL Service Design) A recovery option that is also known as cold standby. Gradual recovery typically uses a portable or fixed facility that has environmental support and network cabling, but no computer systems. The hardware and software are installed as part of the IT service continuity plan. Gradual recovery typically takes more than three days, and may take significantly longer.

guideline

A document describing best practice, which recommends what should be done. Compliance with a guideline is not normally enforced.

See also **standard.**

help desk *

A point of contact for users to log incidents. A help desk is usually more technically focussed than a service desk and does not provide a single point of contact for all interaction. The term help desk is often used as a synonym for service desk.

hierarchic escalation

(ITIL Service Operation) Informing or involving more senior levels of management to assist in an escalation.

high availability

(ITIL Service Design) An approach or design that minimizes or hides the effects of configuration item failure from the users of an IT service. High availability solutions are designed to achieve an agreed level of availability and make use of techniques such as fault tolerance, resilience and fast recovery to reduce the number and impact of incidents.

hot standby

See *fast recovery; immediate recovery.*

identity
(ITIL Service Operation) A unique name that is used to identify a user, person or role. The identity is used to grant rights to that user, person or role. Example identities might be the username SmithJ or the role 'change manager'.

immediate recovery
(ITIL Service Design) A recovery option that is also known as hot standby. Provision is made to recover the IT service with no significant loss of service to the customer. Immediate recovery typically uses mirroring, load balancing and split-site technologies.

impact
(ITIL Service Operation) (ITIL Service Transition) A measure of the effect of an incident, problem or change on business processes. Impact is often based on how service levels will be affected. Impact and urgency are used to assign priority.

impact code *
A category used to represent Impact. Impact codes are often used in incident and problem management. Impact codes may be numbers (for example 1, 2, 3) or words (for example major, minor, catastrophic).

incident
(ITIL Service Operation) An unplanned interruption to an IT service or reduction in the quality of an IT service. Failure of a configuration item that has not yet affected service is also an incident – for example, failure of one disk from a mirror set.

incident management
(ITIL Service Operation) The process responsible for managing the lifecycle of all incidents. Incident management ensures that normal service operation is restored as quickly as possible and the business impact is minimized.

incident record
(ITIL Service Operation) A record containing the details of an incident. Each incident record documents the lifecycle of a single incident.

indirect cost

(ITIL Service Strategy) The cost of providing an IT service which cannot be allocated in full to a specific customer – for example, the cost of providing shared servers or software licences. Also known as overhead.

See also *direct cost.*

information and communications technology (ICT) *

Synonym for information technology (IT). The term ICT is used to emphasise the importance of communication technology.

information security management (ISM)

(ITIL Service Design) The process responsible for ensuring that the confidentiality, integrity and availability of an organization's assets, information, data and IT services match the agreed needs of the business. Information security management supports business security and has a wider scope than that of the IT service provider, and includes handling of paper, building access, phone calls etc. for the entire organization.

See also *security management information system.*

information security management system (ISMS)

(ITIL Service Design) The framework of policy, processes, functions, standards, guidelines and tools that ensures an organization can achieve its information security management objectives.

See also *security management information system.*

information security policy

(ITIL Service Design) The policy that governs the organization's approach to information security management.

information system

See *management information system.*

information technology (IT)

The use of technology for the storage, communication or processing of information. The technology typically includes computers, telecommunications, applications and other software. The information may include business data, voice, images, video etc. Information technology is often used to support business processes through IT services.

informed customer *

A manager within the customer organization who is a specialist in managing and communicating with service providers.
See **business representative.**

infrastructure service

A type of supporting service that provides hardware, network or other data centre components. The term is also used as a synonym for supporting service.

infrastructure *

Synonym for IT infrastructure.

Insourcing

A type of supporting service that provides hardware, network or other data centre components. The term is also used as a synonym for supporting service.

infrastructure management *

Activities that focus on the management of hardware, software, networks, and facilities etc. Infrastructure management activities take place at all stages of the service lifecycle, and include management of the full lifecycle of all IT infrastructure.

integration testing *

Testing of a build, release, IT service or group of IT services, to demonstrate that the parts work correctly together.

Integrity

(ITIL Service Design) A security principle that ensures data and configuration items are modified only by authorized personnel and activities. Integrity considers all possible causes of modification, including software and hardware failure, environmental events, and human intervention.

intelligent customer *

Synonym for informed customer.

interactive voice response (IVR)

(ITIL Service Operation) A form of automatic call distribution that accepts user input, such as key presses and spoken commands, to identify the correct destination for incoming calls.

intermediate recovery
(ITIL Service Design) A recovery option that is also known as warm standby. Intermediate recovery usually uses a shared portable or fixed facility that has computer systems and network components. The hardware and software will need to be configured, and data will need to be restored, as part of the IT service continuity plan. Typical recovery times for intermediate recovery are one to three days.

internal customer
A customer who works for the same business as the IT service provider. See also external customer; internal service provider.

internal metric
A metric that is used within the IT service provider to monitor the efficiency, effectiveness or cost effectiveness of the IT service provider's internal processes. Internal metrics are not normally reported to the customer of the IT service.
See also *external metric.*

internal rate of return (IRR)
(ITIL Service Strategy) A technique used to help make decisions about capital expenditure. It calculates a figure that allows two or more alternative investments to be compared. A larger internal rate of return indicates a better investment.
See also *net present value; return on investment.*

internal service provider
(ITIL Service Strategy) An IT service provider that is part of the same organization as its customer. An IT service provider may have both internal and external customers.
See also *insourcing; Type I service provider; Type II service provider.*

internal sourcing *
Using an internal service provider to manage IT services.
See *service sourcing, type I service provider, Type II service provider.*

internal target *
See *internal metric.*

International Organization for Standardization (ISO)

The International Organization for Standardization (ISO) is the world's largest developer of standards. ISO is a non-governmental organization that is a network of the national standards institutes of 156 countries.
See www.iso.org for further information about ISO.

International Standards Organization

See *International Organization for Standardization.*

internet service provider (ISP)

An external service provider that provides access to the internet. Most ISPs also provide other IT services such as web hosting.

invocation

(ITIL Service Design) Initiation of the steps defined in a plan - for example, initiating the IT service continuity plan for one or more IT services.

Ishikawa diagram

(ITIL Continual Service Improvement) (ITIL Service Operation) A technique that helps a team to identify all the possible causes of a problem. Originally devised by Kaoru Ishikawa, the output of this technique is a diagram that looks like a fishbone.

ISO 9000

A generic term that refers to a number of international standards and guidelines for quality management systems. See www.iso.org for more information.
See also *International Organization for Standardization.*

ISO 9001

An international standard for quality management systems.
See also *ISO 9000; standard.*

ISO/IEC 20000

An international standard for IT service management.

ISO/IEC 27001

(ITIL Continual Service Improvement) (ITIL Service Design) An international specification for information security management. The corresponding code of practice is ISO/IEC 27002.
See also *standard.*

ISO/IEC 27002

(ITIL Continual Service Improvement) An international code of practice for information security management. The corresponding specification is ISO/IEC 27001.
See also *standard.*

IT accounting

See *accounting.*

IT directorate *

Senior management within a service provider, charged with developing and delivering IT services. Most commonly used in UK government departments.
See *IT steering group.*

IT infrastructure

All of the hardware, software, networks, facilities etc. that are required to develop, test, deliver, monitor, control or support applications and IT services. The term includes all of the information technology but not the associated people, processes and documentation.

IT operations

(ITIL Service Operation) Activities carried out by IT operations control, including console management/operations bridge, job scheduling, backup and restore, and print and output management. IT operations is also used as a synonym for service operation.

IT operations control

(ITIL Service Operation) The function responsible for monitoring and control of the IT services and IT infrastructure.
See also o*perations bridge.*

IT operations management

(ITIL Service Operation) The function within an IT service provider that performs the daily activities needed to manage IT services and the supporting IT infrastructure. IT operations management includes IT operations control and facilities management. IT service A service provided by an IT service provider. An IT service is made up of a combination of information technology, people and processes. A customer-facing IT service directly supports the business processes of one or more customers and its service level targets should be defined in a service level agreement. Other IT services, called supporting services, are not directly used by the business but are required by the service provider to deliver customer-facing services.

See also *core service; enabling service; enhancing service; service; service package.*

IT service

A service provided by an IT service provider. An IT service is made up of a combination of information technology, people and processes. A customer-facing IT service directly supports the business processes of one or more customers and its service level targets should be defined in a service level agreement. Other IT services, called supporting services, are not directly used by the business but are required by the service provider to deliver customer-facing services.

See also *core service; enabling service; enhancing service; service; service package.*

IT service continuity management (ITSCM)

(ITIL Service Design) The process responsible for managing risks that could seriously affect IT services. IT service continuity management ensures that the IT service provider can always provide minimum agreed service levels, by reducing the risk to an acceptable level and planning for the recovery of IT services.

IT service continuity plan

(ITIL Service Design) A plan defining the steps required to recover one or more IT services. The plan also identifies the triggers for invocation, people to be involved, communications etc. The IT service continuity plan should be part of a business continuity plan.

IT service management (ITSM)

The implementation and management of quality IT services that meet the needs of the business. IT service management is performed by IT service providers through an appropriate mix of people, process and information technology. See also service management.

IT Service Management Forum (itSMF)

The IT Service Management Forum is an independent organization dedicated to promoting a professional approach to IT service management. The itSMF is a not-forprofit membership organization with representation in many countries around the world (itSMF chapters). The itSMF and its membership contribute to the development of ITIL and associated IT service management standards. See www.itsmf.com for more information.

IT service provider

(ITIL Service Strategy) A service provider that provides IT services to internal or external customers.

IT steering group (ISG)

(ITIL Service Design) (ITIL Service Strategy) A formal group that is responsible for ensuring that business and IT service provider strategies and plans are closely aligned. An IT steering group includes senior representatives from the business and the IT service provider. Also known as IT strategy group or IT steering committee.

ITIL®

A set of best-practice publications for IT service management. Owned by the Cabinet Office (part of HM Government), ITIL gives guidance on the provision of quality IT services and the processes, functions and other capabilities needed to support them. The ITIL framework is based on a service lifecycle and consists of five lifecycle stages (service strategy, service design, service transition, service operation and continual service improvement), each of which has its own supporting publication. There is also a set of complementary ITIL publications providing guidance specific to industry sectors, organization types, operating models and technology architectures.
See www.itilofficialsite.com for more information.

job description

A document that defines the roles, responsibilities, skills and knowledge required by a particular person. One job description can include multiple roles – for example, the roles of configuration manager and change manager may be carried out by one person.

job scheduling

(ITIL Service Operation) Planning and managing the execution of software tasks that are required as part of an IT service. Job scheduling is carried out by IT operations management, and is often automated using software tools that run batch or online tasks at specific times of the day, week, month or year.

K

Kano model
(ITIL Service Strategy) A model developed by Noriaki Kano that is used to help understand customer preferences. The Kano model considers attributes of an IT service grouped into areas such as basic factors, excitement factors, performance factors etc.

Kepner & Tregoe analysis
(ITIL Service Operation) A structured approach to problem solving. The problem is analysed in terms of what, where, when and extent. Possible causes are identified, the most probable cause is tested, and the true cause is verified.

key performance indicator (KPI)
(ITIL Continual Service Improvement) (ITIL Service Design) A metric that is used to help manage an IT service, process, plan, project or other activity. Key performance indicators are used to measure the achievement of critical success factors. Many metrics may be measured, but only the most important of these are defined as key performance indicators and used to actively manage and report on the process, IT service or activity. They should be selected to ensure that efficiency, effectiveness and cost effectiveness are all managed.

knowledge base
(ITIL Service Transition) A logical database containing data and information used by the service knowledge management system.

knowledge management
(ITIL Service Transition) The process responsible for sharing perspectives, ideas, experience and information, and for ensuring that these are available in the right place and at the right time. The knowledge management process enables informed decisions, and improves efficiency by reducing the need to rediscover knowledge.
See also *Data-to-Information-to-Knowledgeto- Wisdom; service knowledge management system.*

known error

(ITIL Service Operation) A problem that has a documented root cause and a workaround. Known errors are created and managed throughout their lifecycle by problem management. Known errors may also be identified by development or suppliers.

known error database (KEDB)

(ITIL Service Operation) A database containing all known error records. This database is created by problem management and used by incident and problem management. The known error database may be part of the configuration management system, or may be stored elsewhere in the service knowledge management system.

known error record

(ITIL Service Operation) A record containing the details of a known error. Each known error record documents the lifecycle of a known error, including the status, root cause and workaround. In some implementations, a known error is documented using additional fields in a problem record. lifecycle The various stages in the life of an IT service, configuration item, incident, problem, change etc. The lifecycle defines the categories for status and the status transitions that are permitted. For example: the lifecycle of an application includes requirements, design, build, deploy, operate, optimize; the expanded incident lifecycle includes detection, diagnosis, repair, recovery and restoration; the lifecycle of a server may include ordered, received, in test, live, disposed etc.

L

lifecycle
The various stages in the life of an IT service, configuration item, incident, problem, change etc. The lifecycle defines the categories for status and the status transitions that are permitted. For example: the lifecycle of an application includes requirements, design, build, deploy, operate, optimize; the expanded incident lifecycle includes detection, diagnosis, repair, recovery and restoration; the lifecycle of a server may include ordered, received, in test, live, disposed etc.

line of service (LOS)
(ITIL Service Strategy) A core service or service package that has multiple service options. A line of service is managed by a service owner and each service option is designed to support a particular market segment.

live
(ITIL Service Transition) Refers to an IT service or other configuration item that is being used to deliver service to a customer.

live environment
(ITIL Service Transition) A controlled environment containing live configuration items used to deliver IT services to customers.

M

maintainability
(ITIL Service Design) A measure of how quickly and effectively an IT service or other configuration item can be restored to normal working after a failure. Maintainability is often measured and reported as MTRS. Maintainability is also used in the context of software or IT service development to mean ability to be changed or repaired easily.

major incident
(ITIL Service Operation) The highest category of impact for an incident. A major incident results in significant disruption to the business.

manageability
An informal measure of how easily and effectively an IT service or other component can be managed.

managed services *
A perspective on IT services which emphasises the fact that they are managed. The term managed services is also used as a synonym for outsourced IT services.

management information
Information that is used to support decision making by managers. Management information is often generated automatically by tools supporting the various IT service management processes. Management information often includes the values of key performance indicators, such as 'percentage of changes leading to incidents' or 'first-time fix rate'.

management information system (MIS)
(ITIL Service Design) A set of tools, data and information that is used to support a process or function. Examples include the availability management information system and the supplier and contract management information system.
See also *service knowledge management system.*

Management of Risk (M_o_R®)
M_o_R includes all the activities required to identify and control the exposure to risk, which may have an impact on the achievement of an organization's business objectives. See www.mor-officialsite.com for more details.

management system
The framework of policy, processes, functions, standards, guidelines and tools that ensures an organization or part of an organization can achieve its objectives. This term is also used with a smaller scope to support a specific process or activity – for example, an event management system or risk management system.
See also *system.*

manual workaround
(ITIL Continual Service Improvement) A workaround that requires manual intervention. Manual workaround is also used as the name of a recovery option in which the business process operates without the use of IT services. This is a temporary measure and is usually combined with another recovery option.

marginal cost
(ITIL Service Strategy) The increase or decrease in the cost of producing one more, or one less, unit of output – for example, the cost of supporting an additional user.

market space
(ITIL Service Strategy) Opportunities that an IT service provider could exploit to meet the business needs of customers. Market spaces identify the possible IT services that an IT service provider may wish to consider delivering.

maturity
(ITIL Continual Service Improvement) A measure of the reliability, efficiency and effectiveness of a process, function, organization etc. The most mature processes and functions are formally aligned to business objectives and strategy, and are supported by a framework for continual improvement.

maturity level
A named level in a maturity model, such as the Carnegie Mellon Capability Maturity Model Integration.

mean time between failures (MTBF)
(ITIL Service Design) A metric for measuring and reporting reliability. MTBF is the average time that an IT service or other configuration item can perform its agreed function without interruption. This is measured from when the configuration item starts working, until it next fails.

mean time between service incidents (MTBSI)

(ITIL Service Design) A metric used for measuring and reporting reliability. It is the mean time from when a system or IT service fails, until it next fails. MTBSI is equal to MTBF plus MTRS.

mean time to repair (MTTR)

The average time taken to repair an IT service or other configuration item after a failure. MTTR is measured from when the configuration item fails until it is repaired. MTTR does not include the time required to recover or restore. It is sometimes incorrectly used instead of mean time to restore service.

mean time to restore service (MTRS)

The average time taken to restore an IT service or other configuration item after a failure. MTRS is measured from when the configuration item fails until it is fully restored and delivering its normal functionality.
See also *maintainability; mean time to repair.*

metric

(ITIL Continual Service Improvement) Something that is measured and reported to help manage a process, IT service or activity.
See also *key performance indicator.*

middleware

(ITIL Service Design) Software that connects two or more software components or applications. Middleware is usually purchased from a supplier, rather than developed within the IT service provider.
See also *commercial off the shelf.*

mission

A short but complete description of the overall purpose and intentions of an organization. It states what is to be achieved, but not how this should be done.
See also *vision.*

model

A representation of a system, process, IT service, configuration item etc. that is used to help understand or predict future behaviour.

modelling

A technique that is used to predict the future behaviour of a system, process, IT service, configuration item etc. Modelling is commonly used in financial management, capacity management and availability management.

monitor control loop

(ITIL Service Operation) Monitoring the output of a task, process, IT service or other configuration item; comparing this output to a predefined norm; and taking appropriate action based on this comparison.

monitoring

(ITIL Service Operation) Repeated observation of a configuration item, IT service or process to detect events and to ensure that the current status is known.

near-shore
(ITIL Service Strategy) Provision of services from a country near the country where the customer is based. This can be the provision of an IT service, or of supporting functions such as a service desk.
See also *offshore; onshore.*

net present value (NPV)
(ITIL Service Strategy) A technique used to help make decisions about capital expenditure. It compares cash inflows with cash outflows. Positive net present value indicates that an investment is worthwhile.
See also *internal rate of return; return on investment.*

normal change
(ITIL Service Transition) A change that is not an emergency change or a standard change. Normal changes follow the defined steps of the change management process.

normal service operation
(ITIL Service Operation) An operational state where services and configuration items are performing within their agreed service and operational levels.

notional charging
(ITIL Service Strategy) An approach to charging for IT services. Charges to customers are calculated and customers are informed of the charge, but no money is actually transferred. Notional charging is sometimes introduced to ensure that customers are aware of the costs they incur, or as a stage during the introduction of real charging.

O

objective
The outcomes required from a process, activity or organization in order to ensure that its purpose will be fulfilled. Objectives are usually expressed as measurable targets. The term is also informally used to mean a requirement.

off the shelf
See *commercial off the shelf.*

Office of Government Commerce (OGC)
OGC (former owner of Best Management Practice) and its functions have moved into the Cabinet Office as part of HM Government.
See www.cabinetoffice.gov.uk

Office of Public Sector Information (OPSI) *
OPSI license the Crown Copyright material used in the ITIL publications. They are a UK government department who provide online access to UK legislation, license the re-use of Crown copyright material, manage the Information Fair Trader Scheme, maintain the Government's Information Asset Register and provide advice and guidance on official publishing and Crown copyright.

offshore
(ITIL Service Strategy) Provision of services from a location outside the country where the customer is based, often in a different continent. This can be the provision of an IT service, or of supporting functions such as a service desk.
See also *near-shore; onshore.*

onshore
(ITIL Service Strategy) Provision of services from a location within the country where the customer is based.
See also *near-shore; offshore.*

operate
To perform as expected. A process or configuration item is said to operate if it is delivering the required outputs. Operate also means to perform one or more operations. For example, to operate a computer is to do the day-to-day operations needed for it to perform as expected.

operation

(ITIL Service Operation) Day-to-day management of an IT service, system or other configuration item. Operation is also used to mean any predefined activity or transaction – for example, loading a magnetic tape, accepting money at a point of sale, or reading data from a disk drive.

operational

The lowest of three levels of planning and delivery (strategic, tactical, operational). Operational activities include the day-to-day or short-term planning or delivery of a business process or IT service management process. The term is also a synonym for live.

operational acceptance *

Part of service acceptance responsible for ensuring that everything needed to support a new or changed service is in place. Operational acceptance often uses a checklist to ensure that all required documentation, processes, tools and training are complete.

operational cost

The cost resulting from running the IT services, which often involves repeating payments – for example, staff costs, hardware maintenance and electricity (also known as current expenditure or revenue expenditure).
See also *capital expenditure.*

operational expenditure (OPEX)

See *operational cost.*

operational level agreement (OLA)

(ITIL Continual Service Improvement) (ITIL Service Design) An agreement between an IT service provider and another part of the same organization. It supports the IT service provider's delivery of IT services to customers and defines the goods or services to be provided and the responsibilities of both parties. For example, there could be an operational level agreement between the IT service provider and a procurement department to obtain hardware in agreed times or between the service desk and a support group to provide incident resolution in agreed times.
See also *service level agreement.*

operations bridge

(ITIL Service Operation) A physical location where IT services and IT infrastructure are monitored and managed.

operations control
See *IT operations control.*

operations management
See *IT operations management.*

opportunity cost
(ITIL Service Strategy) A cost that is used in deciding between investment choices. Opportunity cost represents the revenue that would have been generated by using the resources in a different way. For example, the opportunity cost of purchasing a new server may include not carrying out a service improvement activity that the money could have been spent on. Opportunity cost analysis is used as part of a decision-making process, but opportunity cost is not treated as an actual cost in any financial statement.

optimize
Review, plan and request changes, in order to obtain the maximum efficiency and effectiveness from a process, configuration item, application etc.

organization
A company, legal entity or other institution. The term is sometimes used to refer to any entity that has people, resources and budgets – for example, a project or business unit.

outcome
The result of carrying out an activity, following a process, or delivering an IT service etc. The term is used to refer to intended results as well as to actual results.
See also *objective.*

outsourcing
(ITIL Service Strategy) Using an external service provider to manage IT services.
See also *service sourcing.*

overhead
See *indirect cost.*

P

pain value analysis
(ITIL Service Operation) A technique used to help identify the business impact of one or more problems. A formula is used to calculate pain value based on the number of users affected, the duration of the downtime, the impact on each user, and the cost to the business (if known).

Pareto principle
(ITIL Service Operation) A technique used to prioritize activities. The Pareto principle says that 80% of the value of any activity is created with 20% of the effort. Pareto analysis is also used in problem management to prioritize possible problem causes for investigation.

partnership
A relationship between two organizations that involves working closely together for common goals or mutual benefit. The IT service provider should have a partnership with the business and with third parties who are critical to the delivery of IT services.
See also *value network.*

passive monitoring
(ITIL Service Operation) Monitoring of a configuration item, an IT service or a process that relies on an alert or notification to discover the current status.
See also *active monitoring.*

pattern of business activity (PBA)
(ITIL Service Strategy) A workload profile of one or more business activities. Patterns of business activity are used to help the IT service provider understand and plan for different levels of business activity.
See also *user profile.*

percentage utilization
(ITIL Service Design) The amount of time that a component is busy over a given period of time. For example, if a CPU is busy for 1,800 seconds in a one-hour period, its utilization is 50%.

performance
A measure of what is achieved or delivered by a system, person, team, process or IT service.

performance anatomy *
An approach to organisational culture that integrates, and actively manages, leadership and strategy, people development, technology enablement, performance management and innovation.

performance management
Activities to ensure that something achieves its expected outcomes in an efficient and consistent manner.

pilot
(ITIL Service Transition) A limited deployment of an IT service, a release or a process to the live environment. A pilot is used to reduce risk and to gain user feedback and acceptance.
See also *change evaluation; test.*

plan
A detailed proposal that describes the activities and resources needed to achieve an objective – for example, a plan to implement a new IT service or process. ISO/IEC 20000 requires a plan for the management of each IT service management process.

Plan-Do-Check-Act (PDCA)
(ITIL Continual Service Improvement) A fourstage cycle for process management, attributed to Edward Deming. Plan-Do- Check-Act is also called the Deming Cycle.
Plan – design or revise processes that support the IT services;
Do – implement the plan and manage the processes;
Check – measure the processes and IT services, compare with objectives and produce reports;
Act – plan and implement changes to improve the processes.

planned downtime
(ITIL Service Design) Agreed time when an IT service will not be available. Planned downtime is often used for maintenance, upgrades and testing.
See also *change window; downtime.*

planning
An activity responsible for creating one or more plans – for example, capacity planning.

policy
Formally documented management expectations and intentions. Policies are used to direct decisions, and to ensure consistent and appropriate development and implementation of processes, standards, roles, activities, IT infrastructure etc.

portable facility
(ITIL Service Design) A prefabricated building, or a large vehicle, provided by a third party and moved to a site when needed according to an IT service continuity plan.
See also *fixed facility; recovery option.*

post implementation review (PIR)
A review that takes place after a change or a project has been implemented. It determines if the change or project was successful, and identifies opportunities for improvement.

practice
A way of working, or a way in which work must be done. Practices can include activities, processes, functions, standards and guidelines.
See also *best practice.*

prerequisite for success (PFS)
An activity that needs to be completed, or a condition that needs to be met, to enable successful implementation of a plan or process. It is often an output from one process that is a required input to another process.

pricing
(ITIL Service Strategy) Pricing is the activity for establishing how much customers will be charged.

PRINCE2®
See *PRojects IN Controlled Environments.*

priority
(ITIL Service Operation) (ITIL Service Transition) A category used to identify the relative importance of an incident, problem or change. Priority is based on impact and urgency, and is used to identify required times for actions to be taken. For example, the service level agreement may state that Priority 2 incidents must be resolved within 12 hours.

proactive monitoring
(ITIL Service Operation) Monitoring that looks for patterns of events to predict possible future failures.
See also *reactive monitoring.*

proactive problem management
(ITIL Service Operation) Part of the problem management process. The objective of proactive problem management is to identify problems that might otherwise be missed. Proactive problem management analyses incident records, and uses data collected by other IT service management processes to identify trends or significant problems.

problem
(ITIL Service Operation) A cause of one or more incidents. The cause is not usually known at the time a problem record is created, and the problem management process is responsible for further investigation.

problem management
(ITIL Service Operation) The process responsible for managing the lifecycle of all problems. Problem management proactively prevents incidents from happening and minimizes the impact of incidents that cannot be prevented.

problem record
(ITIL Service Operation) A record containing the details of a problem. Each problem record documents the lifecycle of a single problem.

procedure
A document containing steps that specify how to achieve an activity. Procedures are defined as part of processes.
See also *work instruction.*

process
A structured set of activities designed to accomplish a specific objective. A process takes one or more defined inputs and turns them into defined outputs. It may include any of the roles, responsibilities, tools and management controls required to reliably deliver the outputs. A process may define policies, standards, guidelines, activities and work instructions if they are needed.

process control
The activity of planning and regulating a process, with the objective of performing the process in an effective, efficient and consistent manner.

process manager
A role responsible for the operational management of a process. The process manager's responsibilities include planning and coordination of all activities required to carry out, monitor and report on the process. There may be several process managers for one process – for example, regional change managers or IT service continuity managers for each data centre. The process manager role is often assigned to the person who carries out the process owner role, but the two roles may be separate in larger organizations.

process owner
The person who is held accountable for ensuring that a process is fit for purpose. The process owner's responsibilities include sponsorship, design, change management and continual improvement of the process and its metrics. This role can be assigned to the same person who carries out the process manager role, but the two roles may be separate in larger organizations.

production acceptance *
Synonym for operational acceptance.

production environment
See live environment.

profit centre
(ITIL Service Strategy) A business unit that charges for services provided. A profit centre can be created with the objective of making a profit, recovering costs, or running at a loss. An IT service provider can be run as a cost centre or a profit centre.

pro-forma
A template or example document containing sample data that will be replaced with real values when these are available.

programme
A number of projects and activities that are planned and managed together to achieve an overall set of related objectives and other outcomes.

project

A temporary organization, with people and other assets, that is required to achieve an objective or other outcome. Each project has a lifecycle that typically includes initiation, planning, execution, and closure. Projects are usually managed using a formal methodology such as PRojects IN Controlled Environments (PRINCE2) or the Project Management Body of Knowledge (PMBOK).
See also *charter; project management office; project portfolio.*

project charter

See *charter.*

project evaluation review *

Synonym for post implementation review (PIR), used in the context of a completed project.

Project Management Body of Knowledge (PMBOK) *

A project management standard maintained and published by the Project Management Institute. See www.pmi.org for more information.
See also *PRojects IN Controlled Environments (PRINCE2).*

Project Management Institute (PMI) *

A membership association that advances the project management profession through globally recognized standards and certifications, collaborative communities, an extensive research programme, and professional development opportunities. PMI is a not-for-profit membership organization with representation in many countries around the world. PMI maintains and publishes the Project Management Body of Knowledge (PMBOK). See www.pmi.org for more information.
See also *PRojects IN Controlled Environments (PRINCE2).*

project management office (PMO) *

(ITIL Service Design) (ITIL Service Strategy) A function or group responsible for managing the lifecycle of projects.
See also *charter; project portfolio.*

project portfolio

(ITIL Service Design) (ITIL Service Strategy) A database or structured document used to manage projects throughout their lifecycle. The project portfolio is used to coordinate projects and ensure that they meet their objectives in a cost-effective and timely manner. In larger organizations, the project portfolio is typically defined and maintained by a project management office. The project portfolio is important to service portfolio management as new services and significant changes are normally managed as projects.

See also *charter.*

projected service outage (PSO)

(ITIL Service Transition) A document that identifies the effect of planned changes, maintenance activities and test plans on agreed service levels.

PRojects IN Controlled Environments (PRINCE2)

The standard UK government methodology for project management. See www.princeofficialsite. com for more information.

See also *Project Management Body of Knowledge (PMBOK).*

Q

qualification
(ITIL Service Transition) An activity that ensures that the IT infrastructure is appropriate and correctly configured to support an application or IT service. See also *validation.*

quality
The ability of a product, service or process to provide the intended value. For example, a hardware component can be considered to be of high quality if it performs as expected and delivers the required reliability. Process quality also requires an ability to monitor effectiveness and efficiency, and to improve them if necessary.
See also *quality management system.*

quality assurance (QA)
(ITIL Service Transition) The process responsible for ensuring that the quality of a service, process or other service asset will provide its intended value. Quality assurance is also used to refer to a function or team that performs quality assurance. This process is not described in detail within the core ITIL publications.
See also *service validation and testing.*

quality management system (QMS)
(ITIL Continual Service Improvement) The framework of policy, processes, functions, standards, guidelines and tools that ensures an organization is of a suitable quality to reliably meet business objectives or service levels.
See also *ISO 9000.*

queuing theory *
An analytical modelling technique that models the rate of arrival of requests for resources such as disks, CPUs, servers, services etc. Queuing theory can be used to predict the response times and resource requirements of systems when the throughput or workload changes.

quick win
(ITIL Continual Service Improvement) An improvement activity that is expected to provide a return on investment in a short period of time with relatively small cost and effort.
See also *Pareto principle.*

RACI

(ITIL Service Design) A model used to help define roles and responsibilities. RACI stands for responsible, accountable, consulted and informed.

RAG chart *

A type of SLAM Chart that uses red, amber (or yellow) and green colours to indicate failure, warning and success states.

reactive monitoring

(ITIL Service Operation) Monitoring that takes place in response to an event. For example, submitting a batch job when the previous job completes, or logging an incident when an error occurs.
See also *proactive monitoring.*

real charging

(ITIL Service Strategy) A charging policy where actual money is transferred from the customer to the IT service provider in payment for the delivery of IT services.
See also *notional charging.*

reciprocal arrangement

(ITIL Service Design) A recovery option. An agreement between two organizations to share resources in an emergency – for example, high-speed printing facilities or computer room space.

record

A document containing the results or other output from a process or activity. Records are evidence of the fact that an activity took place and may be paper or electronic – for example, an audit report, an incident record or the minutes of a meeting.

recovery

(ITIL Service Design) (ITIL Service Operation) Returning a configuration item or an IT service to a working state. Recovery of an IT service often includes recovering data to a known consistent state. After recovery, further steps may be needed before the IT service can be made available to the users (restoration).

recovery option

(ITIL Service Design) A strategy for responding to an interruption to service. Commonly used strategies are manual workaround, reciprocal arrangement, gradual recovery, intermediate recovery, fast recovery, and immediate recovery. Recovery options may make use of dedicated facilities or third-party facilities shared by multiple businesses.

recovery point objective (RPO)

(ITIL Service Design) (ITIL Service Operation) The maximum amount of data that may be lost when service is restored after an interruption. The recovery point objective is expressed as a length of time before the failure. For example, a recovery point objective of one day may be supported by daily backups, and up to 24 hours of data may be lost. Recovery point objectives for each IT service should be negotiated, agreed and documented, and used as requirements for service design and IT service continuity plans.

recovery time objective (RTO)

(ITIL Service Design) (ITIL Service Operation) The maximum time allowed for the recovery of an IT service following an interruption. The service level to be provided may be less than normal service level targets. Recovery time objectives for each IT service should be negotiated, agreed and documented. See also ***business impact analysis.***

redundancy

(ITIL Service Design) Use of one or more additional configuration items to provide fault tolerance. The term also has a generic meaning of obsolescence, or no longer needed.

relationship

A connection or interaction between two people or things. In business relationship management, it is the interaction between the IT service provider and the business. In service asset and configuration management, it is a link between two configuration items that identifies a dependency or connection between them. For example, applications may be linked to the servers they run on, and IT services have many links to all the configuration items that contribute to that IT service.

relationship processes

The ISO/IEC 20000 process group that includes business relationship management and supplier management.

release
(ITIL Service Transition) One or more changes to an IT service that are built, tested and deployed together. A single release may include changes to hardware, software, documentation, processes and other components.

release acceptance *
Acceptance of a release at the end of release build and test, before deployment.

release and deployment management
(ITIL Service Transition) The process responsible for planning, scheduling and controlling the build, test and deployment of releases, and for delivering new functionality required by the business while protecting the integrity of existing services.

release identification
(ITIL Service Transition) A naming convention used to uniquely identify a release. The release identification typically includes a reference to the configuration item and a version number – for example, Microsoft Office 2010 SR2.

release management
See *release and deployment management*

release mechanism *
The method for deploying a release to its target environment. A release mechanism may include hardware and software tools as well as procedures.

release package
(ITIL Service Transition) A set of configuration items that will be built, tested and deployed together as a single release. Each release package will usually include one or more release units.

release record
(ITIL Service Transition) A record that defines the content of a release. A release record has relationships with all configuration items that are affected by the release. Release records may be in the configuration management system or elsewhere in the service knowledge management system.

release schedule *
A document that lists all releases and their planned implementation details and dates. The release schedule is published to relevant stakeholders, and forms a significant part of the change schedule.

release unit
(ITIL Service Transition) Components of an IT service that are normally released together. A release unit typically includes sufficient components to perform a useful function. For example, one release unit could be a desktop PC, including hardware, software, licences, documentation etc. A different release unit may be the complete payroll application, including IT operations procedures and user training.

release window
See *change window.*

reliability
(ITIL Continual Service Improvement) (ITIL Service Design) A measure of how long an IT service or other configuration item can perform its agreed function without interruption. Usually measured as MTBF or MTBSI. The term can also be used to state how likely it is that a process, function etc. will deliver its required outputs.
See also *availability.*

remediation
(ITIL Service Transition) Actions taken to recover after a failed change or release. Remediation may include back-out, invocation of service continuity plans, or other actions designed to enable the business process to continue.

remote fix *
Resolution of an incident or problem without support staff visiting the physical location of the failed configuration item.

repair
(ITIL Service Operation) The replacement or correction of a failed configuration item.

request for change (RFC)
(ITIL Service Transition) A formal proposal for a change to be made. It includes details of the proposed change, and may be recorded on paper or electronically. The term is often misused to mean a change record, or the change itself.

request for service *
Synonym for service request.

request fulfilment
(ITIL Service Operation) The process responsible for managing the lifecycle of all service requests.

request model
(ITIL Service Operation) A repeatable way of dealing with a particular category of service request. A request model defines specific agreed steps that will be followed for a service request of this category. Request models may be very simple, with no requirement for authorization (e.g. password reset), or may be more complex with many steps that require authorization (e.g. provision of an existing IT service).
See also *request fulfilment.*

requirement
(reset), or may be more complex with many steps that require authorization (e.g. provision of an existing IT service).
See also *request fulfilment.*

resolution
(ITIL Service Operation) Action taken to repair the root cause of an incident or problem, or to implement a workaround. In ISO/IEC 20000, resolution processes is the process group that includes incident and problem management.

resolution processes
The ISO/IEC 20000 process group that includes incident and problem management.

resource
(ITIL Service Strategy) A generic term that includes IT infrastructure, people, money or anything else that might help to deliver an IT service. Resources are considered to be assets of an organization.
See also *capability; service asset.*

resource capacity management *
Synonym for component capacity management.

response time
A measure of the time taken to complete an operation or transaction. Used in capacity management as a measure of IT infrastructure performance, and in incident management as a measure of the time taken to answer the phone, or to start diagnosis.

responsiveness
A measurement of the time taken to respond to something. This could be response time of a transaction, or the speed with which an IT service provider responds to an incident or request for change etc. restoration of service.

restoration of service
See *restore.*

restore
(ITIL Service Operation) Taking action to return an IT service to the users after repair and recovery from an incident. This is the primary objective of incident management.

retire
(ITIL Service Transition) Permanent removal of an IT service, or other configuration item, from the live environment. Being retired is a stage in the lifecycle of many configuration items.

return on assets (ROA)
(ITIL Service Strategy) A measurement of the profitability of a business unit or organization. Return on assets is calculated by dividing the annual net income by the total value of assets.
See also *return on investment.*

return on investment (ROI)
(ITIL Continual Service Improvement) (ITIL Service Strategy) A measurement of the expected benefit of an investment. In the simplest sense, it is the net profit of an investment divided by the net worth of the assets invested.
See also *net present value; value on investment.*

return to normal
(ITIL Service Design) The phase of an IT service continuity plan during which full normal operations are resumed. For example, if an alternative data centre has been in use, then this phase will bring the primary data centre back into operation, and restore the ability to invoke IT service continuity plans again.

review
An evaluation of a change, problem, process, project etc. Reviews are typically carried out at predefined points in the lifecycle, and especially after closure. The purpose of a review is to ensure that all deliverables have been provided, and to identify opportunities for improvement.
See also *change evaluation; post-implementation review.*

rights
(ITIL Service Operation) Entitlements, or permissions, granted to a user or role - for example, the right to modify particular data, or to authorize a change.

risk
A possible event that could cause harm or loss, or affect the ability to achieve objectives. A risk is measured by the probability of a threat, the vulnerability of the asset to that threat, and the impact it would have if it occurred. Risk can also be defined as uncertainty of outcome, and can be used in the context of measuring the probability of positive outcomes as well as negative outcomes.

risk analysis *
Synonym for risk assessment.

risk assessment
The initial steps of risk management: analysing the value of assets to the business, identifying threats to those assets, and evaluating how vulnerable each asset is to those threats. Risk assessment can be quantitative (based on numerical data) or qualitative.

risk management
The process responsible for identifying, assessing and controlling risks. Risk management is also sometimes used to refer to the second part of the overall process after risks have been identified and assessed, as in 'risk assessment and management'. This process is not described in detail within the core ITIL publications.
See also *risk assessment.*

risk reduction measure *
Action taken to reduce the likelihood or impact of a risk.
See *control.*

role

A set of responsibilities, activities and authorities assigned to a person or team. A role is defined in a process or function. One person or team may have multiple roles – for example, the roles of configuration manager and change manager may be carried out by a single person. Role is also used to describe the purpose of something or what it is used for.

rollout *

Synonym for deployment. Most often used to refer to complex or phased deployments or deployments to multiple locations.

root cause

(ITIL Service Operation) The underlying or original cause of an incident or problem. root cause analysis (RCA).

root cause analysis (RCA)

(ITIL Service Operation) An activity that identifies the root cause of an incident or problem. Root cause analysis typically concentrates on IT infrastructure failures.
See also *service failure analysis. running costs.*

running costs

See *operational costs.*

Sarbanes-Oxley (SOX)
US law that regulates financial practice and corporate governance.

scalability
The ability of an IT service, process, configuration item etc. to perform its agreed function when the workload or scope changes.

scope
The boundary or extent to which a process, procedure, certification, contract etc. applies. For example, the scope of change management may include all live IT services and related configuration items; the scope of an ISO/IEC 20000 certificate may include all IT services delivered out of a named data centre.

script *
A sequence of predefined steps. For example a diagnostic script used during incident or problem management, or an automated computer script executed as part of system management or IT operations.

second level support *
Synonym for second-line support.

second-line support
(ITIL Service Operation) The second level in a hierarchy of support groups involved in the resolution of incidents and investigation of problems. Each level contains more specialist skills, or has more time or other resources.

security
See *information security management.*

security management
See *information security management.*

security management information system (SMIS)
(ITIL Service Design) A set of tools, data and information that is used to support information security management. The security management information system is part of the information security management system. See also service knowledge management system.

security policy
See *information security policy.*

separation of concerns (SoC)
An approach to designing a solution or IT service that divides the problem into pieces that can be solved independently. This approach separates what is to be done from how it is to be done.

server
(ITIL Service Operation) A computer that is connected to a network and provides software functions that are used by other computers.

service
A means of delivering value to customers by facilitating outcomes customers want to achieve without the ownership of specific costs and risks. The term 'service' is sometimes used as a synonym for core service, IT service or service package.
See also *utility; warranty.*

service acceptance criteria (SAC)
(ITIL Service Transition) A set of criteria used to ensure that an IT service meets its functionality and quality requirements and that the IT service provider is ready to operate the new IT service when it has been deployed.
See also *acceptance.*

service achievement *
Synonym for service level.

service analytics
(ITIL Service Strategy) A technique used in the assessment of the business impact of incidents. Service analytics models the dependencies between configuration items, and the dependencies of IT services on configuration items.

service asset
Any resource or capability of a service provider.
See also *asset.*

service asset and configuration management (SACM)

(ITIL Service Transition) The process responsible for ensuring that the assets required to deliver services are properly controlled, and that accurate and reliable information about those assets is available when and where it is needed. This information includes details of how the assets have been configured and the relationships between assets.

See also *configuration management system.*

service capacity management (SCM)

(ITIL Continual Service Improvement) (ITIL Service Design) The sub-process of capacity management responsible for understanding the performance and capacity of IT services. Information on the resources used by each IT service and the pattern of usage over time are collected, recorded and analysed for use in the capacity plan.

See also *business capacity management; component capacity management.*

service catalogue

(ITIL Service Design) (ITIL Service Strategy) A database or structured document with information about all live IT services, including those available for deployment. The service catalogue is part of the service portfolio and contains information about two types of IT service: customer-facing services that are visible to the business; and supporting services required by the service provider to deliver customer-facing services.

See also *customer agreement portfolio; service catalogue management.*

service catalogue management

(ITIL Service Design) The process responsible for providing and maintaining the service catalogue and for ensuring that it is available to those who are authorized to access it.

service change

See *change.*

service charter

(ITIL Service Design) (ITIL Service Strategy) A document that contains details of a new or changed service. New service introductions and significant service changes are documented in a charter and authorized by service portfolio management. Service charters are passed to the service design lifecycle stage where a new or modified service design package will be created. The term charter is also used to describe the act of authorizing the work required by each stage of the service lifecycle with respect to the new or changed service.

See also *change proposal; service portfolio; service catalogue.*

service continuity management

See *IT service continuity management.*

service contract

(ITIL Service Strategy) A contract to deliver one or more IT services. The term is also used to mean any agreement to deliver IT services, whether this is a legal contract or a service level agreement.
See also *customer agreement portfolio.*

service culture

A customer-oriented culture. The major objectives of a service culture are customer satisfaction and helping customers to achieve their business objectives.

service design

(ITIL Service Design) A stage in the lifecycle of a service. Service design includes the design of the services, governing practices, processes and policies required to realize the service provider's strategy and to facilitate the introduction of services into supported environments. Service design includes the following processes: design coordination, service catalogue management, service level management, availability management, capacity management, IT service continuity management, information security management, and supplier management. Although these processes are associated with service design, most processes have activities that take place across multiple stages of the service lifecycle.
See also *design.*

service design package (SDP)

(ITIL Service Design) Document(s) defining all aspects of an IT service and its requirements through each stage of its lifecycle. A service design package is produced for each new IT service, major change or IT service retirement.

service desk

(ITIL Service Operation) The single point of contact between the service provider and the users. A typical service desk manages incidents and service requests, and also handles communication with the users.

service failure analysis (SFA)

(ITIL Service Design) A technique that identifies underlying causes of one or more IT service interruptions. Service failure analysis identifies opportunities to improve the IT service provider's processes and tools, and not just the IT infrastructure. It is a timeconstrained, project-like activity, rather than an ongoing process of analysis.

service hours

(ITIL Service Design) An agreed time period when a particular IT service should be available. For example, 'Monday-Friday 08:00 to 17:00 except public holidays'. Service hours should be defined in a service level agreement.

service improvement plan (SIP)

(ITIL Continual Service Improvement) A formal plan to implement improvements to a process or IT service.

service knowledge management system (SKMS)

(ITIL Service Transition) A set of tools and databases that is used to manage knowledge, information and data. The service knowledge management system includes the configuration management system, as well as other databases and information systems. The service knowledge management system includes tools for collecting, storing, managing, updating, analysing and presenting all the knowledge, information and data that an IT service provider will need to manage the full lifecycle of IT services.
See also *knowledge management.*

service level

Measured and reported achievement against one or more service level targets. The term is sometimes used informally to mean service level target.

service level agreement (SLA)

(ITIL Continual Service Improvement) (ITIL Service Design) An agreement between an IT service provider and a customer. A service level agreement describes the IT service, documents service level targets, and specifies the responsibilities of the IT service provider and the customer. A single agreement may cover multiple IT services or multiple customers.
See also *operational level agreement.*

service level management (SLM)

(ITIL Service Design) The process responsible for negotiating achievable service level agreements and ensuring that these are met. It is responsible for ensuring that all IT service management processes, operational level agreements and underpinning contracts are appropriate for the agreed service level targets. Service level management monitors and reports on service levels, holds regular service reviews with customers, and identifies required improvements.

service level package (SLP)

See *service option.* service level requirement (SLR)

service level requirement (SLR)

(ITIL Continual Service Improvement) (ITIL Service Design) A customer requirement for an aspect of an IT service. Service level requirements are based on business objectives and used to negotiate agreed service level targets.

service level target

(ITIL Continual Service Improvement) (ITIL Service Design) A commitment that is documented in a service level agreement. Service level targets are based on service level requirements, and are needed to ensure that the IT service is able to meet business objectives. They should be SMART, and are usually based on key performance indicators.

service lifecycle

An approach to IT service management that emphasizes the importance of coordination and control across the various functions, processes and systems necessary to manage the full lifecycle of IT services. The service lifecycle approach considers the strategy, design, transition, operation and continual improvement of IT services. Also known as service management lifecycle.

service maintenance objective (SMO)

(ITIL Service Operation) The expected time that a configuration item will be unavailable due to planned maintenance activity.

service management

A set of specialized organizational capabilities for providing value to customers in the form of services.

service management lifecycle

See *service lifecycle.*

service manager

A generic term for any manager within the service provider. Most commonly used to refer to a business relationship manager, a process manager or a senior manager with responsibility for IT services overall.

service model

(ITIL Service Strategy) A model that shows how service assets interact with customer assets to create value. Service models describe the structure of a service (how the configuration items fit together) and the dynamics of the service (activities, flow of resources and interactions). A service model can be used as a template or blueprint for multiple services.

service operation

(ITIL Service Operation) A stage in the lifecycle of a service. Service operation coordinates and carries out the activities and processes required to deliver and manage services at agreed levels to business users and customers. Service operation also manages the technology that is used to deliver and support services. Service operation includes the following processes: event management, incident management, request fulfilment, problem management, and access management. Service operation also includes the following functions: service desk, technical management, IT operations management, and application management. Although these processes and functions are associated with service operation, most processes and functions have activities that take place across multiple stages of the service lifecycle. See also *operation.*

service option

(ITIL Service Design) (ITIL Service Strategy) A choice of utility and warranty offered to customers by a core service or service package. Service options are sometimes referred to as service level packages.

service outage analysis *

Synonym for service failure analysis (SFA).

service owner

(ITIL Service Strategy) A role responsible for managing one or more services throughout their entire lifecycle. Service owners are instrumental in the development of service strategy and are responsible for the content of the service portfolio.
See also *business relationship management.*

service package
(ITIL Service Strategy) Two or more services that have been combined to offer a solution to a specific type of customer need or to underpin specific business outcomes. A service package can consist of a combination of core services, enabling services and enhancing services. A service package provides a specific level of utility and warranty. Customers may be offered a choice of utility and warranty through one or more service options.
See also *IT service.*

service pipeline
(ITIL Service Strategy) A database or structured document listing all IT services that are under consideration or development, but are not yet available to customers. The service pipeline provides a business view of possible future IT services and is part of the service portfolio that is not normally published to customers.

service portfolio
(ITIL Service Strategy) The complete set of services that is managed by a service provider. The service portfolio is used to manage the entire lifecycle of all services, and includes three categories: service pipeline (proposed or in development), service catalogue (live or available for deployment), and retired services.
See also *customer agreement portfolio; service portfolio management.*

service portfolio management (SPM)
(ITIL Service Strategy) The process responsible for managing the service portfolio. Service portfolio management ensures that the service provider has the right mix of services to meet required business outcomes at an appropriate level of investment. Service portfolio management considers services in terms of the business value that they provide.

service potential
(ITIL Service Strategy) The total possible value of the overall capabilities and resources of the IT service provider.

service provider
(ITIL Service Strategy) An organization supplying services to one or more internal customers or external customers. Service provider is often used as an abbreviation for IT service provider. See also Type I service provider; Type II service provider; Type III service provider.

service provider interface (SPI)
(ITIL Service Strategy) An interface between the IT service provider and a user, customer, business process or supplier. Analysis of service provider interfaces helps to coordinate end-to-end management of IT services.

service reporting
(ITIL Continual Service Improvement) Activities that produce and deliver reports of achievement and trends against service levels. The format, content and frequency of reports should be agreed with customers.

service request
(ITIL Service Operation) A formal request from a user for something to be provided – for example, a request for information or advice; to reset a password; or to install a workstation for a new user. Service requests are managed by the request fulfilment process, usually in conjunction with the service desk. Service requests may be linked to a request for change as part of fulfilling the request.

service sourcing
(ITIL Service Strategy) The strategy and approach for deciding whether to provide a service internally, to outsource it to an external service provider, or to combine the two approaches. Service sourcing also means the execution of this strategy.
See also *insourcing; internal service provider; outsourcing.*

service strategy
(ITIL Service Strategy) A stage in the lifecycle of a service. Service strategy defines the perspective, position, plans and patterns that a service provider needs to execute to meet an organization's business outcomes. Service strategy includes the following processes: strategy management for IT services, service portfolio management, financial management for IT services, demand management, and business relationship management. Although these processes are associated with service strategy, most processes have activities that take place across multiple stages of the service lifecycle.

service transition

(ITIL Service Transition) A stage in the lifecycle of a service. Service transition ensures that new, modified or retired services meet the expectations of the business as documented in the service strategy and service design stages of the lifecycle. Service transition includes the following processes: transition planning and support, change management, service asset and configuration management, release and deployment management, service validation and testing, change evaluation, and knowledge management. Although these processes are associated with service transition, most processes have activities that take place across multiple stages of the service lifecycle.

See also *transition.*

service validation and testing

(ITIL Service Transition) The process responsible for validation and testing of a new or changed IT service. Service validation and testing ensures that the IT service matches its design specification and will meet the needs of the business.

service valuation

(ITIL Service Strategy) A measurement of the total cost of delivering an IT service, and the total value to the business of that IT service. Service valuation is used to help the business and the IT service provider agree on the value of the IT service.

serviceability

(ITIL Continual Service Improvement) (ITIL Service Design) The ability of a third-party supplier to meet the terms of its contract. This contract will include agreed levels of reliability, maintainability and availability for a configuration item.

seven-step improvement process

(ITIL Continual Service Improvement) The process responsible for defining and managing the steps needed to identify, define, gather, process, analyse, present and implement improvements. The performance of the IT service provider is continually measured by this process and improvements are made to processes, IT services and IT infrastructure in order to increase efficiency, effectiveness and cost effectiveness. Opportunities for improvement are recorded and managed in the CSI register.

severity code *
A category used to represent severity of a problem or known error.
See *impact code.*

shared service unit
See *Type II service provider.*

shift
(ITIL Service Operation) A group or team of people who carry out a specific role for a fixed period of time. For example, there could be four shifts of IT operations control personnel to support an IT service that is used 24 hours a day.

simulation modelling
(ITIL Continual Service Improvement) (ITIL Service Design) A technique that creates a detailed model to predict the behaviour of an IT service or other configuration item. A simulation model is often created by using the actual configuration items that are being modelled with artificial workloads or transactions. They are used in capacity management when accurate results are important. A simulation model is sometimes called a performance benchmark.
See also *analytical modelling; modelling.*

single point of contact
(ITIL Service Operation) Providing a single consistent way to communicate with an organization or business unit. For example, a single point of contact for an IT service provider is usually called a service desk.

single point of failure (SPOF)
(ITIL Service Design) Any configuration item that can cause an incident when it fails, and for which a countermeasure has not been implemented. A single point of failure may be a person or a step in a process or activity, as well as a component of the IT infrastructure.
See also *failure.*

SLAM chart
(ITIL Continual Service Improvement) A service level agreement monitoring chart is used to help monitor and report achievements against service level targets. A SLAM chart is typically colour-coded to show whether each agreed service level target has been met, missed or nearly missed during each of the previous 12 months.

SMART

(ITIL Continual Service Improvement) (ITIL Service Design) An acronym for helping to remember that targets in service level agreements and project plans should be specific, measurable, achievable, relevant and time-bound.

snapshot

(ITIL Continual Service Improvement) (ITIL Service Transition) The current state of a configuration item, process or any other set of data recorded at a specific point in time. Snapshots can be captured by discovery tools or by manual techniques such as an assessment.
See also *baseline; benchmark.*

software asset management (SAM)

(ITIL Service Transition) The process responsible for tracking and reporting the use and ownership of software assets throughout their lifecycle. Software asset management is part of an overall service asset and configuration management process. This process is not described in detail within the core ITIL publications.

Software Process Improvement and Capability dEtermination (SPICE) *

A framework for the assessment of software development processes, that evolved into ISO/IEC 15504. SPICE is partly based on the Capability Maturity Model Integration.

source

See *service sourcing.*

spares store *

One or more physical locations, set aside for the storage of hardware spares, maintained at the same revision and quality as configuration items (CIs) in the live environment.

specification

A formal definition of requirements. A specification may be used to define technical or operational requirements, and may be internal or external. Many public standards consist of a code of practice and a specification. The specification defines the standard against which an organization can be audited.

stakeholder

A person who has an interest in an organization, project, IT service etc. Stakeholders may be interested in the activities, targets, resources or deliverables. Stakeholders may include customers, partners, employees, shareholders, owners etc.

See also **RACI.**

standard

A mandatory requirement. Examples include ISO/IEC 20000 (an international standard), an internal security standard for Unix configuration, or a government standard for how financial records should be maintained. The term is also used to refer to a code of practice or specification published by a standards organization such as ISO or BSI.

See also **guideline.**

standard change

(ITIL Service Transition) A pre-authorized change that is low risk, relatively common and follows a procedure or work instruction – for example, a password reset or provision of standard equipment to a new employee. Requests for change are not required to implement a standard change, and they are logged and tracked using a different mechanism, such as a service request.

See also **change model.**

standard operating procedures (SOP)

(ITIL Service Operation) Procedures used by IT operations management.

standby

(ITIL Service Design) Used to refer to resources that are not required to deliver the live IT services, but are available to support IT service continuity plans. For example, a standby data centre may be maintained to support hot standby, warm standby or cold standby arrangements.

statement of requirements (SOR)

(ITIL Service Design) A document containing all requirements for a product purchase, or a new or changed IT service.

See also **terms of reference.**

status

The name of a required field in many types of record. It shows the current stage in the lifecycle of the associated configuration item, incident, problem etc.

status accounting
(ITIL Service Transition) The activity responsible for recording and reporting the lifecycle of each configuration item.

storage management
(ITIL Service Operation) The process responsible for managing the storage and maintenance of data throughout its lifecycle.

strategic
(ITIL Service Strategy) The highest of three levels of planning and delivery (strategic, tactical, operational). Strategic activities include objective setting and long-term planning to achieve the overall vision.

strategic asset
(ITIL Service Strategy) Any asset that provides the basis for core competence, distinctive performance or sustainable competitive advantage, or which allows a business unit to participate in business opportunities. Part of service strategy is to identify how IT can be viewed as a strategic asset rather than an internal administrative function.

strategy
(ITIL Service Strategy) A strategic plan designed to achieve defined objectives.

strategy management for IT services
(ITIL Service Strategy) The process responsible for defining and maintaining an organization's perspective, position, plans and patterns with regard to its services and the management of those services. Once the strategy has been defined, strategy management for IT services is also responsible for ensuring that it achieves its intended business outcomes.

super user
(ITIL Service Operation) A user who helps other users, and assists in communication with the service desk or other parts of the IT service provider. Super users are often experts in the business processes supported by an IT service and will provide support for minor incidents and training.

supplier

(ITIL Service Design) (ITIL Service Strategy) A third party responsible for supplying goods or services that are required to deliver IT services. Examples of suppliers include commodity hardware and software vendors, network and telecom providers, and outsourcing organizations.
See also *supply chain; underpinning contract.*

supplier and contract management information system (SCMIS)

(ITIL Service Design) A set of tools, data and information that is used to support supplier management.
See also *service knowledge management system.*

supplier management

(ITIL Service Design) The process responsible for obtaining value for money from suppliers, ensuring that all contracts and agreements with suppliers support the needs of the business, and that all suppliers meet their contractual commitments.
See also *supplier and contract management information system.*

supply chain

(ITIL Service Strategy) The activities in a value chain carried out by suppliers. A supply chain typically involves multiple suppliers, each adding value to the product or service.
See also *value network.*

support group

(ITIL Service Operation) A group of people with technical skills. Support groups provide the technical support needed by all of the IT service management processes.
See also *technical management.*

support hours

(ITIL Service Design) (ITIL Service Operation) The times or hours when support is available to the users. Typically these are the hours when the service desk is available. Support hours should be defined in a service level agreement, and may be different from service hours. For example, service hours may be 24 hours a day, but the support hours may be 07:00 to 19:00.

supporting service

(ITIL Service Design) An IT service that is not directly used by the business, but is required by the IT service provider to deliver customer-facing services (for example, a directory service or a backup service). Supporting services may also include IT services only used by the IT service provider. All live supporting services, including those available for deployment, are recorded in the service catalogue along with information about their relationships to customer-facing services and other CIs.

SWOT analysis

(ITIL Continual Service Improvement) A technique that reviews and analyses the internal strengths and weaknesses of an organization and the external opportunities and threats that it faces. SWOT stands for strengths, weaknesses, opportunities and threats.

system

A number of related things that work together to achieve an overall objective. For example: a computer system including hardware, software and applications; a management system, including the framework of policy, processes, functions, standards, guidelines and tools that are planned and managed together – for example, a quality management system; or a database management system or operating system that includes many software modules which are designed to perform a set of related functions.

system management

The part of IT service management that focuses on the management of IT infrastructure rather than process. tactical The middle of three levels of planning and delivery (strategic, tactical, operational). Tactical activities include the medium-term plans required to achieve specific objectives, typically over a period of weeks to months.

tactical
The middle of three levels of planning and delivery (strategic, tactical, operational). Tactical activities include the medium-term plans required to achieve specific objectives, typically over a period of weeks to months.

task *
An activity or set of activities that might be defined as part of a process. Each task should be documented in a procedure or work instruction.

technical management
(ITIL Service Operation) The function responsible for providing technical skills in support of IT services and management of the IT infrastructure. Technical management defines the roles of support groups, as well as the tools, processes and procedures required.

technical observation (TO)
(Continual Service Improvement) A technique used in Service Improvement, Problem investigation and Availability Management. Technical support staff meet to monitor the behaviour and Performance of an IT Service and make recommendations for improvement.

technical service *
Synonym for supporting service.

technical support
See *technical management.*

tension metrics
(ITIL Continual Service Improvement) A set of related metrics, in which improvements to one metric have a negative effect on another. Tension metrics are designed to ensure that an appropriate balance is achieved.

terms of reference (TOR)
(ITIL Service Design) A document specifying the requirements, scope, deliverables, resources and schedule for a project or activity.

test
(ITIL Service Transition) An activity that verifies that a configuration item, IT service, process etc. meets its specification or agreed requirements.
See also *acceptance; service validation and testing.*

test environment
(ITIL Service Transition) A controlled environment used to test configuration items, releases, IT services, processes etc.

third party
(ITIL Service Transition) A person, organization or other entity that is not part of the service provider's own organization and is not a customer – for example, a software supplier or a hardware maintenance company. Requirements for third parties are typically specified in contracts that underpin service level agreements.
See also *underpinning contract.*

third-line support
(ITIL Service Operation) The third level in a hierarchy of support groups involved in the resolution of incidents and investigation of problems. Each level contains more specialist skills, or has more time or other resources.

threat
A threat is anything that might exploit a vulnerability. Any potential cause of an incident can be considered a threat. For example, a fire is a threat that could exploit the vulnerability of flammable floor coverings. This term is commonly used in information security management and IT service continuity management, but also applies to other areas such as problem and availability management.

threshold
The value of a metric that should cause an alert to be generated or management action to be taken. For example, 'Priority 1 incident not solved within four hours', 'More than five soft disk errors in an hour', or 'More than 10 failed changes in a month'.

throughput
(ITIL Service Design) A measure of the number of transactions or other operations performed in a fixed time – for example, 5,000 e-mails sent per hour, or 200 disk I/Os per second.

tied users *

Users who have no choice other than to use the IT services provided by their internal service provider.
See *untied users.*

total cost of ownership (TCO)

(ITIL Service Strategy) A methodology used to help make investment decisions. It assesses the full lifecycle cost of owning a configuration item, not just the initial cost or purchase price.
See also *total cost of utilization.*

total cost of utilization (TCU)

(ITIL Service Strategy) A methodology used to help make investment and service sourcing decisions. Total cost of utilization assesses the full lifecycle cost to the customer of using an IT service.
See also *total cost of ownership.*

total quality management (TQM)

(ITIL Continual Service Improvement) A methodology for managing continual improvement by using a quality management system. Total quality management establishes a culture involving all people in the organization in a process of continual monitoring and improvement.

transaction

A discrete function performed by an IT service – for example, transferring money from one bank account to another. A single transaction may involve numerous additions, deletions and modifications of data. Either all of these are completed successfully or none of them is carried out.

transfer cost

(ITIL Service Strategy) A cost type which records expenditure made on behalf of another part of the organization. For example, the IT service provider may pay for an external consultant to be used by the finance department and transfer the cost to them. The IT service provider would record this as a transfer cost.

transition

(ITIL Service Transition) A change in state, corresponding to a movement of an IT service or other configuration item from one lifecycle status to the next.

transition planning and support
(ITIL Service Transition) The process responsible for planning all service transition processes and coordinating the resources that they require.

trend analysis
(ITIL Continual Service Improvement) Analysis of data to identify time-related patterns. Trend analysis is used in problem management to identify common failures or fragile configuration items, and in capacity management as a modelling tool to predict future behaviour. It is also used as a management tool for identifying deficiencies in IT service management processes.

trouble ticket *
A term used by some service management tools to refer to an incident, a problem or any work item that can be assigned to support staff.

tuning
The activity responsible for planning changes to make the most efficient use of resources. Tuning is most commonly used in the context of IT services and components. Tuning is part of capacity management, which also includes performance monitoring and implementation of the required changes. Tuning is also called optimization, particularly in the context of processes and other nontechnical resources.

Type I service provider
(ITIL Service Strategy) An internal service provider that is embedded within a business unit. There may be several Type I service providers within an organization.

Type II service provider
(ITIL Service Strategy) An internal service provider that provides shared IT services to more than one business unit. Type II service providers are also known as shared service units.

Type III service provider
(ITIL Service Strategy) A service provider that provides IT services to external customers.

underpinning contract (UC)
(ITIL Service Design) A contract between an IT service provider and a third party. The third party provides goods or services that support delivery of an IT service to a customer. The underpinning contract defines targets and responsibilities that are required to meet agreed service level targets in one or more service level agreements.

unit cost
(ITIL Service Strategy) The cost to the IT service provider of providing a single component of an IT service. For example, the cost of a single desktop PC, or of a single transaction.

untied users *
Users who can choose whether to use the services provided by an internal service provider or to purchase services from another source.
See *tied users.*

urgency
(ITIL Service Design) (ITIL Service Transition) A measure of how long it will be until an incident, problem or change has a significant impact on the business. For example, a high-impact incident may have low urgency if the impact will not affect the business until the end of the financial year. Impact and urgency are used to assign priority.

usability
(ITIL Service Design) The ease with which an application, product or IT service can be used. Usability requirements are often included in a statement of requirements.

use case
(ITIL Service Design) A technique used to define required functionality and objectives, and to design tests. Use cases define realistic scenarios that describe interactions between users and an IT service or other system.

user
A person who uses the IT service on a dayto- day basis. Users are distinct from customers, as some customers do not use the IT service directly.

user forum *

A formal meeting of users that is usually organised by the service provider to measure satisfaction and to gain feedback to help with continual improvement.

user profile (UP)

(ITIL Service Strategy) A pattern of user demand for IT services. Each user profile includes one or more patterns of business activity.

utility

(ITIL Service Strategy) The functionality offered by a product or service to meet a particular need. Utility can be summarized as 'what the service does', and can be used to determine whether a service is able to meet its required outcomes, or is 'fit for purpose'. The business value of an IT service is created by the combination of utility and warranty.

See also *service validation and testing.*

validation

(ITIL Service Transition) An activity that ensures a new or changed IT service, process, plan or other deliverable meets the needs of the business. Validation ensures that business requirements are met even though these may have changed since the original design.

See also *acceptance; qualification; service validation and testing; verification.*

value chain

(ITIL Service Strategy) A sequence of processes that creates a product or service that is of value to a customer. Each step of the sequence builds on the previous steps and contributes to the overall product or service.

See also *value network.*

value for money

An informal measure of cost effectiveness. Value for money is often based on a comparison with the cost of alternatives.

See also *cost benefit analysis.*

value network

(ITIL Service Strategy) A complex set of relationships between two or more groups or organizations. Value is generated through exchange of knowledge, information, goods or services.

See also *partnership; value chain.*

value on investment (VOI)

(ITIL Continual Service Improvement) A measurement of the expected benefit of an investment. Value on investment considers both financial and intangible benefits.

See also *return on investment.*

variable cost

(ITIL Service Strategy) A cost that depends on how much the IT service is used, how many products are produced, the number and type of users, or something else that cannot be fixed in advance.

variable cost dynamics *
A technique used to understand how overall costs are impacted by the many complex variable elements that contribute to the provision of IT services.

variance
The difference between a planned value and the actual measured value. Commonly used in financial management, capacity management and service level management, but could apply in any area where plans are in place.

verification
(ITIL Service Transition) An activity that ensures that a new or changed IT service, process, plan or other deliverable is complete, accurate, reliable and matches its design specification.
See also *acceptance; validation; service validation and testing.*

verification and audit
(ITIL Service Transition) The activities responsible for ensuring that information in the configuration management system is accurate and that all configuration items have been identified and recorded. Verification includes routine checks that are part of other processes – for example, verifying the serial number of a desktop PC when a user logs an incident. Audit is a periodic, formal check.

version
(ITIL Service Transition) A version is used to identify a specific baseline of a configuration item. Versions typically use a naming convention that enables the sequence or date of each baseline to be identified. For example, payroll application version 3 contains updated functionality from version 2.

vision
A description of what the organization intends to become in the future. A vision is created by senior management and is used to help influence culture and strategic planning.
See also *mission.*

vital business function (VBF)
(ITIL Service Design) Part of a business process that is critical to the success of the business. Vital business functions are an important consideration of business continuity management, IT service continuity management and availability management.

vulnerability

A weakness that could be exploited by a threat - for example, an open firewall port, a password that is never changed, or a flammable carpet. A missing control is also considered to be a vulnerability. warm standby
See *intermediate recovery.*

warm standby
See *intermediate recovery.*

warranty
(ITIL Service Strategy) Assurance that a product or service will meet agreed requirements. This may be a formal agreement such as a service level agreement or contract, or it may be a marketing message or brand image. Warranty refers to the ability of a service to be available when needed, to provide the required capacity, and to provide the required reliability in terms of continuity and security. Warranty can be summarized as 'how the service is delivered', and can be used to determine whether a service is 'fit for use'. The business value of an IT service is created by the combination of utility and warranty.
See also *service validation and testing.*

waterline *
A way of presenting the service catalogue. Customer-facing services are made visible to the customer and are considered to be above the waterline, Supporting services are not made visible and are considered to be below the waterline. This metaphor is based on the fact that the parts of an ocean liner below the waterline are the engines and propulsion system, and these are not normally visible to passengers.

work in progress (WIP)
A status that means activities have started but are not yet complete. It is commonly used as a status for incidents, problems, changes etc.

work instruction
A document containing detailed instructions that specify exactly what steps to follow to carry out an activity. A work instruction contains much more detail than a procedure and is only created if very detailed instructions are needed.

work order
A formal request to carry out a defined activity. Work orders are often used by change management and by release and deployment management to pass requests to technical management and application management functions.

workaround

(ITIL Service Operation) Reducing or eliminating the impact of an incident or problem for which a full resolution is not yet available – for example, by restarting a failed configuration item. Workarounds for problems are documented in known error records. Workarounds for incidents that do not have associated problem records are documented in the incident record.

workflow diagram *

A diagram that represents a process or activity. Workflow diagrams show steps, timings and exchanges of information with other processes or activities.

workload

The resources required to deliver an identifiable part of an IT service. Workloads may be categorized by users, groups of users, or functions within the IT service. This is used to assist in analysing and managing the capacity, performance and utilization of configuration items and IT services. The term is sometimes used as a synonym for throughput.

workload management *

Activities in capacity management that predict workload trends and analyse their likely effects.

Abbreviations List

ACD	automatic call distribution
AM	availability management
AMIS	availability management information system
ASP	application service provider
AST	agreed service time
BCM	business continuity management
BCP	business continuity plan
BIA	business impact analysis
BMP	Best Management Practice
BRM	business relationship manager
BSI	British Standards Institution
CAB	change advisory board
CAPEX	capital expenditure
CCM	component capacity management
CFIA	component failure impact analysis
CI	configuration item
CMDB	configuration management database
CMIS	capacity management information system
CMM	capability maturity model
CMMI	Capability Maturity Model Integration
CMS	configuration management system
COBIT	Control OBjectives for Information and related Technology
COTS	commercial off the shelf
CSF	critical success factor
CSI	continual service improvement
CTI	computer telephony integration
DIKW	Data-to-Information-to-Knowledge-to-Wisdom
DML	definitive media library
ECAB	emergency change advisory board
ELS	early life support
eSCM-CL	eSourcing Capability Model for Client Organizations
eSCM-SP	eSourcing Capability Model for Service Providers
FTA	fault tree analysis
ICT	information and communications technology

IRR	internal rate of return
ISG	IT steering group
ISM	information security management
ISMS	information security management system
ISO	International Organization for Standardization
ISP	internet service provider
IT	information technology
ITSCM	IT service continuity management
ITSM	IT service management
itSMF	IT Service Management Forum
IVR	interactive voice response
KEDB	known error database
KPI	key performance indicator
LOS	line of service
MIS	management information system
M_o_R	Management of Risk
MTBF	mean time between failures
MTBSI	mean time between service incidents
MTRS	mean time to restore service
MTTR	mean time to repair
NPV	net present value
OLA	operational level agreement
OPEX	operational expenditure
PBA	pattern of business activity
PDCA	Plan-Do-Check-Act
PFS	prerequisite for success
PIR	post-implementation review
PMBOK	Project Management Body of Knowledge
PMI	Project Management Institute
PMO	project management office
PRINCE2	PRojects IN Controlled Environments
PSO	projected service outage
QA	quality assurance
QMS	quality management system
RACI	responsible, accountable, consulted and informed
RAG	red, amber, green. See RAG chart *
RCA	root cause analysis
RFC	request for change

ROA	return on assets
ROI	return on investment
RPO	recovery point objective
RTO	recovery time objective
SAC	service acceptance criteria
SACM	service asset and configuration management
SAM	software asset management
SCM	service capacity management
SCMIS	supplier and contract management information system
SDP	service design package
SFA	service failure analysis
SIP	service improvement plan
SKMS	service knowledge management system
SLA	service level agreement
SLM	service level management
SLP	service level package
SLR	service level requirement
SMART	specific, measurable, achievable, relevant and time-bound
SMIS	security management information system
SMO	service maintenance objective
SoC	separation of concerns
SOP	standard operating procedure
SOR	statement of requirements
SOX	Sarbanes-Oxley (US law)
SPI	service provider interface
SPICE	Software Process Improvement and Capability dEtermination
SPM	service portfolio management
SPOF	single point of failure
TCO	total cost of ownership
TCU	total cost of utilization
TO	technical observation
TOR	terms of reference
TQM	total quality management
UC	underpinning contract
UP	user profile
VBF	vital business function
VOI	value on investment
WIP	work in progress

Further Guidance and Contact Points

itSMF Ltd (itSMF UK)
150 Wharfedale Road
Winnersh Triangle
Wokingham
Berkshire RG41 5RB
United Kingdom
Tel: +44(0)118 918 6500
Fax: +44(0)118 969 9749
E-mail: publications@itsmf.co.uk
www.itsmf.co.uk

TSO
PO Box 29
Norwich NR3 1GN
United Kingdom
Tel: +44(0) 870 600 5522
Fax: +44(0) 870 600 5533
E-mail: customer.services@tso.co.uk
www.tso.co.uk

British Standards Institution
389 Chiswick High Road
London W4 4AL
United Kingdom
Tel: +44(0)208 996 9001
Fax: +44(0)208 996 7001
E-mail: info@bsi-global.com
www.bsi-global.com

The Cabinet Office (Best
Management Practice)
Rosebery Court
St Andrews Business Park
Norwich NR7 0HS
United Kingdom
Tel: +44(0)1603 704567
Fax: +44(0)1603 704817
www.cabinetoffice.gov.uk

APM Group Limited
Sword House
Totteridge Road
High Wycombe
Buckinghamshire
HP13 6DG
Tel: +44 (0) 1494 452 450
Fax: +44 (0) 1494 459 559
E-mail: servicedesk@apmgroup.co.uk
www.apmgroup.co.uk

About itSMF

The itSMF is the only truly independent and internationally recognized forum for IT Service Management professionals worldwide. This not-for-profit organization is a prominent player in the on-going development and promotion of IT Service Management "best practice", standards and qualifications and has been since 1991.

Globally, the itSMF now boasts over 6000 member companies, blue chip and public sector alike, covering in excess of 70,000 individuals spread over 40+ international chapters.

Each chapter is a separate legal entity and is largely autonomous. The UK chapter has over 9,000 members: it offers a flourishing annual conference, online bookstore, regular regional meetings and special interest groups and numerous other benefits for members. Its website is at www.itsmf.co.uk.

There is a separate international entity, itSMF International, that provides an overall steering and support function to existing and emerging chapters. It has its own website at **www.itsmf.org.**